THE WORLD
ACCORDING TO

THE WORLD ACCORDING TO

CLARE FLOWERS

MICHAEL O'MARA BOOKS LIMITED

First published in Great Britain in 2003 by
Michael O'Mara Books Limited
9 Lion Yard
Tremadoc Road
London SW4 7NQ

A CIP catalogue record for this book is available from
the British Library

ISBN 1-84317-031-0   .

1 3 5 7 9 10 8 6 4 2

Designed and typeset by Design 23

Printed and bound in Finland by WS Bookwell, Juva

CONTENTS

For Jonny and Ben

INTRODUCTION

In July 1953, a young man called Elvis Presley did something that would change his life, and everyone else's, for generations to come. Aged eighteen, six weeks after leaving school, and carrying the little guitar that had been his constant companion since his eleventh birthday, he walked along to 706 Union Avenue and through the door of Memphis Recording Service, home of Sam Phillips's nascent Sun label.

He paid $3.98 plus tax to make his first one-off record; next time, they would pay him. Whether or not, as he later claimed, the disc was 'a surprise for my mother', or if it was in the hope of being discovered professionally by Sam Phillips, it was certainly the first serious step by a sweet southern boy with music in his bones towards a level of stardom he could never have imagined. He would be bigger than James Dean, bigger than Marlon Brando. He would be King.

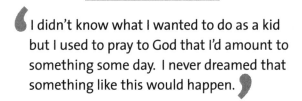
I didn't know what I wanted to do as a kid but I used to pray to God that I'd amount to something some day. I never dreamed that something like this would happen.

It was less than a decade since the end of the Second World War, and there was something new in the air. The films *On the Waterfront* (1954), starring Brando, and *Rebel Without a Cause* (1955), starring Dean, were to articulate a new kind of angst brewing in the soul of American youth, soon to spread the world over. This was the brief window of time in the twentieth century that spawned a new phenomenon: the teenager. And Elvis Presley was its avatar.

Like many great avatars, his was a humble beginning. He was born Elvis Aron Presley on 8 January, 1935 in a two-room shack built by his father, Vernon, in the poorest part of Tupelo, Mississippi, the younger by half-an-hour of twins. The other boy, christened Jesse Garon, was still-born. It is well-documented that a surviving twin in these circumstances can suffer from a sense of loss for the rest of his or her life. Did the young Elvis miss his brother? Certainly towards the end of his life he did become obsessed with contacting the spirit of his lost twin beyond the grave.

The absence ever after of Jesse Garon may account for Elvis's extraordinarily close relationship with his mother, Gladys. She doted on him – he was unquestionably a mother's boy. They even communicated much of the time in a baby language of their own invention. Both parents struggled to give their only son everything they could, and he, in turn, gave them everything they could want, as soon as he was in a position to do so.

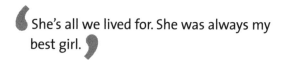

She's all we lived for. She was always my best girl.

Family was the cornerstone of Elvis's life – in addition to his own flesh and blood, he sought as an adult to create a surrogate family to cushion him as his career developed; he only ever had one mother but his Svengali-like manager, Colonel Tom Parker, became a surrogate father, and the 'Memphis Mafia', the group of men he kept around him throughout his adult life, essentially functioned as brothers, although as happens in Greek tragedy, some would eventually betray him.

The urge to make his parents' lives more comfortable was one of the driving forces behind his quest to make a career out of singing – it would have taken a lot longer had he become an electrician, as Gladys and Vernon originally hoped, or a cop, as he himself fantasized. His dream was one day to buy his parents a house, and move them on from run-down rented places on the wrong side of the tracks. The dream was to be realized much sooner than he expected.

Elvis was the kind of son every mother would love to have – polite, thoughtful and caring. When he proudly brought home his first pay packet from his job at a machinist's shop, he handed the contents straight to Gladys without a second thought. There was no question about who wore the trousers in the family, especially where Elvis was concerned. Gladys was the dominant parent and the primary influence. Vernon was a gentle but ineffectual man whose attempts to hold down paid work never came to much. Yet, as the precious only child, Elvis flourished in a climate of love and nurturing created by both of them. His sharp wit and dry humour were his father's, but from Gladys he inherited the softer, more feminine side of his character – expressed in his fondness even as an adult for creative dressing, make-up, soft toys and his favourite colour, pink – and probably his appreciation of women.

Elvis genuinely liked women. He delighted in their company, loved to please them, amuse them, entertain them. He enjoyed their conversation and listening to what they had to say. At least the younger Elvis did.

' Elvis never was a Casanova-type, or libertine. He was more like a pleasant high school date. '
NATALIE WOOD

He would go on to become something of a love machine. He was generous, buying his women expensive gifts, but he was also possessive and could be jealous.

His upbringing, poor though it was – Vernon and Gladys did, however, succeed in bettering their lot to some extent while Elvis was growing up – sustained him emotionally and spiritually. The Presleys were an extended family and various cousins, uncles and aunts visited the small household regularly, some of them musical. There were singsongs, mostly hillbilly and country. And at some point the family acquired a radio which broadened Elvis's musical education to encompass blues and opera. But it was at church every week that Elvis first began to appreciate music. The First Assembly Church of God in Tupelo was charismatic in style and, as a faithful attender with his parents, he was steeped from babyhood in the glorious gospel that resounded through the tiny building. He never lost his love for it. He recorded several gospel albums which won him three Grammy awards. At the height of his fifties' fame, he would sit at the piano and sing gospel with his parents and whoever else might be around the house after an adrenaline-fuelled concert or a day's filming.

When the Presleys upped sticks and moved in 1948 from Tupelo to Memphis in search of a better life, they settled close to Beale Street, heart of the blues. Here the young Elvis heard the music of BB King, Arthur 'Big Boy' Crudup, Howlin' Wolf and other legends, alive and dead, and took to buying clothes from the Lansky Brothers' emporium on Beale – source of the distinctive early Presley look that was unlike anyone else's and drew taunts on the streets before he became famous.

And the look was all-important. Elvis, who didn't drink or smoke and loved his mother above all else, was a good boy who looked like a bad boy – in other words, a young girl's dream. And he knew just how to work girls up into unprecedented levels of hysteria. From his earliest concerts, cutting his teeth at small clubs round Memphis and in Texas in 1954, the singer with a voice like sweet, dark Tupelo honey and a way with body language that sent the girls wild and set the establishment raging, cut a controversial figure on stage. Would the girls have been quite so hysterical if he had sported a crew-cut and cowboy shirt or a sober suit and tie? Possibly not. To his fans in that conservative era, Elvis was a taste of forbidden fruit – sex. This man was sex incarnate. Sexuality seeped through his every pore: the girls could hear the promise of danger in his voice and they sure could see it in his bumpings, thrustings, sneerings and grindings on stage. Elvis wore black, maybe jazzed up with a wicked flash of pink or a sparkle of gold. Throughout his performing life, from the early, spivvy matador's outfits, through his black leather biker phase to the spangled Vegas vulgarity of the white satin jumpsuits he favoured towards the end, his wardrobe was an essential element of the chemistry that went into the making of the King.

But before the King was ever crowned, he was a little princeling who had his first taste of performing in public at the age of ten, when his teacher suggested to his parents that he enter a children's talent contest at the Mississipi-Alabama Fair and Dairy Show – a big gig for a small boy. He sang *a cappella* the sentimental, bathetic 'Old Shep', about a dead pet, and won a prize. During the next ten years, secure in the bosom of his highly protective, close-knit family, he would develop his talent for singing, learn how to play the guitar and piano, and expand his knowledge of music to an encyclopaedic level.

Then at twenty, he would emerge into the public eye like a butterfly, truly gorgeous to behold and making a sound that would set the world on fire. It was a world that was waiting for something, even if it didn't quite know what that something was. What it got was rock and roll and an artist who would earn his title of King with eighteen Number One hits, RCA record sales of more than $1 billion, thirty-three films and the biggest concert in history – more than a billion people around the world watched and listened via satellite when he performed in Honolulu in January 1973.

But, like the grimmer fairy tales, there was no happy ending. Somewhere along the line, perhaps starting in 1957 with the death of his mother, and his stint in the army when he started taking drugs, the dream began to sour. It wasn't long before a lifetime of high-cholesterol home cooking and junk food took its toll and Elvis started getting flabby, then ran to fat. A regime of crash diets weakened his system. His anti-drink and drugs stance was forgotten as he started taking vast cocktails of medication and developed addictions. The drugs distorted his perceptions of himself and the world around him. His innate need to search for spiritual truth and meaning conflicted with the drugged-up, hermetic lifestyle he led in the King's compound at Graceland, and found expression in an increasingly bizarre array of New Age 'ologies'. Ultimately, when not performing, he spent much of his time holed up in his bachelor fantasy bedroom, bloated, stoned and incoherent, until, aged only forty-two, he died an appropriately tragic rock and roll death – face down on the bathroom floor in a pool of his own vomit. Gladys's heart would have broken, had she been alive to see it. Any mother's would.

But the King is not dead. His influence lives on, as does his music. He is the planet's most impersonated celebrity. People claim that he is not really dead and to have spotted him living quietly in such-and-such a town. People who weren't born when he died in 1977 are captivated by his voice. He can still have hits, as he did in 2002 with the remixed 'A Little Less Conversation'. Elvis was rock and roll's first true star and is still worshipped by millions. But he was also a god that turned into a monster, who in the end devoured himself.

❛Every time I think that I'm getting old, and gradually going to the grave, something else happens. ❜

BORN TO BE KING

I'm not "the King" – Christ is the King. I'm just an entertainer.

When Gladys Love Smith met Vernon Elvis Presley in 1933 at the evangelical First Assembly of God Church in East Tupelo, where her uncle was a preacher, she was twenty-one, he four years younger. Vernon was blond and handsome but immature, and not much of a catch as a breadwinner. Unambitious, he had no trade and little application, working his way through a succession of unskilled jobs, unable to hold any of them down for long. On the other hand, Gladys, who was no beauty but definitely pretty with delicate features, slaved for her wages on twelve-hour shifts at a clothing factory. But there must have been love – their relationship would survive numerous traumas, including Vernon's imprisonment, evictions, chronic poverty and Gladys's obsessive love for her only son. They married with little ceremony in June 1933, after borrowing the $3 licence fee from friends and running away with another couple to another town to tie the knot.

It was no shotgun wedding: Elvis Aron Presley was born nineteen months later at approximately 4.30 am on 8 January, 1935 under the sign of Capricorn. According to astrology, in which Elvis would one day take an interest, this was a baby destined to be introspective but naturally witty, persistent in his determination to realize his dreams and ambitions, and drawn to music. Capricorns often become entertainers. His stillborn identical twin, Jesse Garon, was buried in an unmarked grave in Priceville cemetery, near the two-room wooden shack built by Vernon on Old Saltillo Road, East Tupelo. The glorious blue-eyed good looks that would become iconic were inherited from mixed stock: Scottish, Cherokee and, possibly, Jewish – as an adult he would take to wearing a star of David. Elvis – Vernon's middle name – is thought to be Norse, meaning 'All Wise'. It is also an anagram of 'lives' as in 'Elvis lives'.

After a difficult pregnancy and birth, Gladys was told that there would be no more children and so lavished her maternal affection on baby Elvis. When he was two, catastrophe struck – although the family would survive it, the incident would cause them grief and shame for years to come. Vernon, along with his brother-in-law, Travis Smith, and another man, Luther Gable, was convicted for fraud after changing the sum on a cheque for the sale of a pig from $3 to $8, and sentenced to three years in prison. Although he was released early, after only eight months, and his wife and son had visited every weekend, by the time he got out the bond between Gladys and Elvis was immutable – they even communicated in their own exclusive baby language. However, while it is not uncommon for immature men to feel usurped in their wife's affections by their first-born, Vernon, who had to all intents and purposes been the older Gladys's 'baby' until their son was born, doesn't seem to have exhibited jealousy at being relegated to second place in her affections. Indeed, he was himself always a doting father.

As the focus of all this smother love, the little boy thrived. Elvis was Gladys's little man, her adored prince. He called his mama 'Baby' or 'Satnin'', the meaning of which can only be guessed at, though it may derive from satin, the sheeny fabric that is soft to the touch and pleasant to stroke, almost like skin; in their tactile, affectionate relationship, feet or 'footies', were 'sooties'. She fed him up on the best they could afford: his favourite burned bacon, mashed potatoes, biscuits and what is known in the South as thickenin' gravy – not made with meat juices, but a gluey sauce based on cornflour – and eggs that had to be as tough as rubber before he would touch them. She taught him manners and how to comb his hair to greased perfection, a habit he never lost.

As they moved from home to home, Gladys did her best to create a cosy, insular world for the three of them. Elvis, who had inherited his father's dirty-blonde hair, had few playmates until he entered his teens – his mama was his best friend, though she didn't spare the rod when she thought it necessary; she believed that there was a place for discipline when it came to keeping Elvis on the path she deemed right. He was a shy child, torn between wanting to have fun with other boys and keeping Gladys happy.

> ' My mama never let me out of her sight.
> I couldn't go down to the creek with the
> other kids. Sometimes, when I was little,
> I used to run off. Mama would whip me, and
> I thought she didn't love me. '

Accounts of when Elvis started school vary but he was either five or six, and walked daily with Gladys the half-mile to East Tupelo Consolidated. Vernon was in and out of work and the family was often in debt but there was always enough money to provide Elvis with the comics he enjoyed. There were Smith and Presley relatives around, too, but church was a vital focus for the family.

> ' I believe in the Bible. I believe that all good
> things come from God. I don't believe I'd sing
> the way I do if God hadn't wanted me to.
> My voice is God's will, not mine. '

At the First Assembly Church, which had outgrown the meeting tent it had started up in and was now housed in a simple one-storey wooden building, he was exposed to the charismatic, demonstrative worship of pentecostalism: fundamentalist hellfire and brimstone sermons, speaking in 'tongues' and the gospel singing – though diluted white gospel rather than the pure, deeper black gospel sound he would hear much later on – that would be a primary influence on his musical career. Elvis loved to join in and when he was

❝ not more than two years old, he would slide down off my lap, run into the aisle and scramble up to the platform. He would stand looking at the choir and trying to sing with them. ❞   GLADYS PRESLEY

Elvis's first public performance gave no hint of the consummate musician he would become but it did presage his ability to please a crowd. When he was ten, his teacher, Mrs Grimes, recommended that Elvis be entered into a children's talent show at the Mississippi-Alabama Fair and Dairy Show. Without a musical accompaniment, and standing on a chair so that he could reach the microphone, the little boy sang 'Old Shep', a syrupy country ballad about a dead dog, which went down so well with the crowd that it won him second prize.

Still, he was no prodigy – Elvis's gifts would reveal themselves slowly. For his eleventh birthday, the present he most wanted was a bicycle. In fact, his parents couldn't afford one that year and instead he got, as it turned out, the best present of his life – a child-sized six-string guitar. Vernon's brother Vester showed him some basic chords and Elvis got hold of an instruction book; then, frustrated by its limitations, he sought out the approachable new pastor at the church. Frank Smith, who was only ten years older and a fairly accomplished guitarist, was happy to expand Elvis's chord and fingering repertoire and encouraged him to perform for the congregation during Sunday service.

The Presleys were still not settled, though, and in 1946 left East Tupelo for Tupelo proper, a move downmarket, although they would move to a better part of town within a year. Vernon had a job as a delivery man and Elvis went to a new school, Milam Junior High. Soon he was consumed by music and the urge to know and learn more. The radio was always on at home, tuned to a country music station, or – in that still segregated era – a black station that played blues masters like BB King, Howlin' Wolf and Sonny Boy Williamson, as well as the gospel to which Elvis was so deeply drawn. For a boy as obsessed by music as he was, and at such a young age, it must have made an enormous impression when he was lucky enough to meet a real professional musician. One of his classmates, James Ausborn, had an older brother who was a Tupelo country star. Mississippi Slim broadcast weekly on Saturdays at the local radio station, WELO, and Elvis used to beg Jimmy to take him along to the studio where they were allowed to hang out before and during the show. Sometimes the artist would patiently spend time with his brother's wide-eyed little buddy, showing him chords and teaching him the occasional new song. Elvis was a quick study. Throughout his life, he found it easy to learn words and music quickly. As an adult he would be able to remember verbatim and recite in full Abraham Lincoln's Gettysburg speech which he had learned at school.

Elvis and his guitar were now inseparable and he started taking it to school, where he would entertain classmates at lunchtime, whether they were appreciative or not. It was noticed by his family, teachers and friends that the boy had developed a habit, or tic, of drumming his fingers on the table or against his leg, as if to some internal beat only he could hear. They might have lived in a poor part of town and have had little cash to spare but in the small nest he shared with Vernon and Gladys, Elvis was probably having a reasonably happy childhood. He may not have had much in the way of material possessions or toys but he was never deprived of love.

However, in the peripatetic existence the Presleys led at that time, the biggest and most dramatic move was about to come. In September 1948, Gladys and Vernon sold off their furniture and, just after their son had started the autumn term at school, packed themselves, their clothes and whatever else they could stuff into an eleven-year-old banger that had seen better days, and made for Memphis – and, they must have hoped, better prospects in the big city.

For the first seven months – the coldest of the year – life was tough; home was yet another slummy dump, then another – a single bedsit in a rundown house for all three of them, with a single hotplate for Gladys to cook on. But salvation was just round the corner. Postwar, public housing was a social ideal in America, as it was in Britain. Lauderdale Courts was a local authority development of neat apartments with all the basic mod cons. As with most public housing, there was a points system and, given the dire circumstances in which they were living, the Presleys totted up enough points to be allocated an apartment in September 1949, a year after settling in the city. It wasn't brand new but number 328 had two bedrooms, a sitting room, a kitchen and a bathroom, all for $35 a month which Vernon could easily afford on his paint company wages. They seemed to be set, though Vernon's now-divorced mother, Minnie Mae – always 'Dodger' to Elvis – also moved in with them; it meant another mouth to feed but, to the Presleys, blood was always thicker than water.

Elvis was attending LC Humes High, from where he would eventually graduate in 1953. Interestingly, although his grades were reasonable, he didn't distinguish himself academically; however, it is clear from his aptitude for memorizing songs and film scripts and the dry, ready wit he would eventually exhibit that he was no dummy. As an adult he didn't read much, but the books he did enjoy were serious and demanding, as were his favourite films, and he returned to them over and over again. It may have been that the only thing that really interested him at school was music, and his studies were simply to be endured, although tellingly, he got his best marks for English. Certainly his parents were keen for him to have a proper education: the move to Memphis was made at the weekend so he wouldn't have to miss a single day of school. And Gladys still walked her fourteen-year-old son to the corner nearest the entrance of LC Humes every morning. Did he squirm, as most boys of that age would, at the idea of being spotted with mama by his classmates?

At school, he was shy and never one of the lads. He was still a new boy, after all, and in the brutal Darwinian environment that is the average high-school, he found it hard to fit in. Perhaps in a bid to take part and find his feet, he started working in the school library and later joined the

Reserve Officers Training Corps (ROTC); despite the non-conformist image he would soon begin to develop, he enjoyed dressing up in his military uniform. His cousin Gene Smith, Gladys's nephew, who had also moved to Memphis along with his family and various other relatives, was there to fulfil the essential role of best friend, and without straying too far from the apartment and causing Gladys to worry, there was plenty to do: soda fountains, ice-cream parlours, a cinema, a swimming pool and a record store which would soon become a regular haunt. It wasn't long before he made friends in his building–boys he cycled and played football with after school and at weekends. To add to the family income, he got a job as a theatre usher in the evenings, but Gladys soon made him quit because of the hours. There would be other jobs, too, outside school hours, that helped provide extra cash to spend on his burgeoning interest in clothes.

At fifteen, in the throes of adolescence and its attendant hormone surges, Elvis's idiosyncratic and highly creative personality began to emerge, despite a nasty case of acne. And there was a new excitement on the horizon: girls. Elvis might not have been the most sophisticated boy about town but he was cute enough, or so the girls thought. His first girlfriend was Betty McMann or McMahan, a neighbour at Lauderdale Courts.

It was a typical teenage romance; there were dates at the movies and evenings spent hanging out on the lawn outside their building where, on warm summer nights, Elvis would play his guitar serenading her and any of the neighbours who might be listening. Soon, his attention switched to another girl, Billie Wardlaw, who also lived on his block. Elvis was popular with the neighbourhood mothers, too, thanks to his shy manner and pleasant ways, not to mention his talent for knocking out a selection of charming ballads. These two teenage girls were the first of many women in Elvis's life – he was never short of female company, especially once he had blossomed into the glorious Adonis he became in his twenties. But, interestingly, Gladys doesn't seem to have minded at all. It was never a case of 'no woman will ever be good enough for my precious son'. Nor did she apparently ever see his girlfriends as a threat to her relationship with him – instead she welcomed them into her home and forged friendships with several.

Meanwhile Elvis perfected his combing technique, which he was now using daily to sculpt his increasingly long dirty-blonde hair into a moulded, slicked DA, and honed his chord repertoire. These skills were joined by a new one: driving. Elvis got his licence not long after his sixteenth birthday and, by the following year, when Vernon was in a position to buy a ten-year-old Lincoln, Elvis had *carte blanche* to drive it whenever he liked. Even so, well-trained by Gladys to stay close to home, this teenager's turf was a small patch of territory. He was drawn increasingly to Beale Street, home of the blues and in those days very much a black area, and the location of Lansky Brothers' clothing store. This was a sartorial Mecca to Elvis – the place where he would forge his look – swapping the turned-up jeans and checked shirts that most of his peers wore for a style borrowed from the more flamboyant black characters and musicians he saw in the area. It would be half a century before 'bling-bling' and 'ghetto fabulous' became recognized terms, but Elvis coveted the extreme cuts and colours of the more *outré* lines stocked by Lansky's.

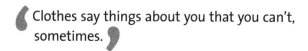

Clothes say things about you that you can't, sometimes.

So where did he get it from, the urge to dress so differently from his peers, most of whom mocked him mercilessly for it? He favoured big, shiny ballooning pants, high-waisted and narrowed at the ankle like the zoot suit pants of the forties, with a flashy insert stripe in lime green or yellow. To top it off, there would be a garish shirt, worn with the collar turned up and out. Had it been thirty years later, no one would have batted an eyelid. But in the early fifties, with his greasy quiff, he stood out like a sore thumb, especially in a poor white neighbourhood in the ultra-conservative Bible belt. In his iconoclastic biography, *Elvis*, Albert Goldman suggests that his inspiration came from the dynamic young actor Tony Curtis, who had appeared in a 1949 film about Brooklyn street gangs, *City Across the River*, in which the actor wore 'a gleaming flawlessly shaped DA with a gleaming forelock…a charming and slightly girlish sort of "bubie boy" who is good with his fists but very sweet and speaks in a sing-song pattern that sounds like baby talk. If ever a film was designed to speak to a young man's condition and temperament, this was the picture for Elvis Presley.' This was a potent image for a shy, baby-talking mama's boy with chronic pimples who must have aspired to a certain masculine toughness and a street *savoir faire*.

If Elvis did borrow his look from a fictional fantasy from the silver screen, it didn't go down well in the redneck reality that was LC Humes High. If you wanted to be one of the good ol' boys, even if only on the football pitch, it didn't do to be different. When he tried out for the school football team in 1951, a mob of players ganged up on him, backed him into a corner and, amid threats and taunts, announced that they were going to cut his cherished long hair. Whether they would have actually gone through with it is impossible to know, but he was saved from finding out by one of the team's toughest, biggest players: Red West, a star player who became a friend and later one of the Memphis Mafia, stepped in and stopped the bullies. But Elvis didn't make the team anyway – the coach said he'd have to get rid of the DA and sideburns and he refused. No matter how much he might have wanted to play football, the image he had so carefully constructed was more important to him. It was the outward badge of his inner aspirations to be and do something different, even if he wasn't sure what; he wasn't about to conform to other people's expectations just for an easy life. The mama's boy was beginning to grow up to be his own man and within a couple of years something would happen that would give his confidence a boost and send his stock, though not his marks, rising at school.

One of his teachers had heard him play his guitar at the class picnic and been impressed. She also noticed that he attracted a crowd round him and asked him to appear at the school concert in the spring of 1953. It was a competition – the act that drew most applause would win. He wore a borrowed red shirt and once again sang 'Old Shep', the bathetic ballad that had won him a prize as a ten-year-old, this time with years of practice under his belt and a guitar under his arm. The audience loved it and this time clapped him into first place – he might be an oddball, but at least he was their oddball.

❝ Nobody knew I sang. I wasn't popular in school. I wasn't dating anybody. In the eleventh grade they entered me in another talent show. I came out and did two songs and heard people kind of rumbling and whispering. I was amazed at how popular I was after that. ❞

His confidence buoyed, Elvis became a regular visitor to local blues clubs and holy-roller-style gospel singing sessions at Ellis Auditorium, the biggest hall in the area; this was white, not black gospel, but the groups on the bill – notably the Blackwood Brothers – were highly adept at whipping up the audience of thousands into a frenzy. At these singalongs he also met and talked to musicians. His musical education was continuing at various tangents, sometimes unexpected ones; he was now listening to classical music on the radio, as well as country, blues and gospel.

> *I had records by Mario Lanza when I was seventeen, eighteen years old. I would listen to the Metropolitan Opera. I just loved music. Music period.*

Things were less good at home – he was working nights and either falling asleep in class or truanting from school, so his grades began to go down. Then, because Gladys had started working as a nursing assistant, the Presleys' income was deemed to be above the maximum allowed at Lauderdale Courts. They were told by the housing department that they would have to go. In January of 1953, shortly after Elvis's eighteenth birthday, they packed up and left. After four years of relative stability, the family had managed to better themselves by dint of hard work, according to the rules of the American dream. But now they were back in lodgings, just like the old days except that now they could afford two rooms instead of one. After brief stints in two different places across town, they settled into a reasonable apartment in a converted Victorian house not far from Lauderdale Courts. It would be a pivotal year for Elvis: Vernon finally managed to buy the car which afforded the teenager a certain freedom and the simple pleasure his better-off peers enjoyed, cruising the streets and beyond the city boundaries. There was also the prom to look forward to, and the culmination of every pupil's high-school career – graduation.

Biographers are divided over whether or not Elvis actually took a girl to the senior prom that summer. Albert Goldman says that, after Billie Wardlaw, he never dated again until his twenties. But in his seminal life of Elvis, *Last Train to Memphis*, the first of a two-part biography, Peter Guralnick says he had been dating a girl called Regis Vaughan, fourteen, since February of that year and that he escorted her to the social event that is a rite of passage for every American high-school student. Elvis is said to have worn a shiny suit to the prom – unlikely to have been of a conservative cut – but didn't dance because he didn't know how to. Elvis's attempts at dancing would never be strictly ballroom.

He graduated from LC Humes High on 3 June 1953, majoring in shop (a technical subject involving wood and metalwork), history and English. His parents must have been extraordinarily proud to see the culmination of their efforts to bring him up 'right', and no doubt his diploma was framed and hung on the wall *chez* Presley. Elvis was not like his father – he didn't even draw breath, never mind feel entitled to take it easy for a week or two. The next day he went out and got himself a job, not the first step in a conventional career plan but something to keep him busy and earn him a wage, at MB Parker machinist's shop. Just six weeks later, he parked his truck, picked up his guitar and walked through the door of Memphis Recording Service, where Sam Phillips ran the Sun record label. He paid his dollars and cut an acetate disc: 'My Happiness' on the A-side and 'That's When Your Heartaches Begin' on the B-side. It was his first tentative step towards making his dreams of being a professional singer a reality – though he could not have known just what kind of singer he would become. And he certainly had no idea of the extraordinary potential that lay inside him, almost – but not quite – ready to be unleashed.

STARS IN HIS EYES

Elvis and the Sun label would be perfect for each other, even if Sam Phillips didn't realize it at first. He was no ordinary music industry operator but a man ahead of his time. The industry was divided: black and white – people and music. Then there was country; hillbilly; blues; rhythm and blues; bluegrass; gospel; pop. A former radio engineer and disc jockey, Phillips loved the music that emanated from black culture and wanted to break down some of those boundaries, musically at least. He detested the division that existed at the core of Deep South society and, after starting up the label in 1950, had begun to make a name as a white man keen to record black artists. An acute ear for quality and a finger on the pulse of the times would lead him to record Jerry Lee Lewis, Carl Perkins, Johnny Cash, BB King and Roy Orbison, as well as the Memphis teenager who would one day be crowned King of Rock and Roll.

So was Elvis's visit to the Memphis Recording Service studio at 706 Union Avenue a few weeks after graduation really meant as a surprise for Gladys, as he later claimed? It seems unlikely; her birthday had been in April. The remark may have been made to deflect attention from a more likely reason: that he secretly hoped Sam Phillips might hear him and spot his talent. If so, his dream was certainly to come true, though not right away.

> ❝ I was an overnight sensation. A year after they heard me the first time, they called me back. ❞

The ballads on the two sides of the disc, for which he paid around $4, gave no hint of the depth of the talent that was fermenting inside him but was not quite ready for public consumption. Afterwards, Sam Phillips's business partner, Marion Keisker, wrote down Elvis's name, address and the number belonging to his next-door neighbour – the Presleys still had no phone. Crucially, she made a note: 'Good ballad singer. Hold.' She duly filed it for future reference and stored the sound of his voice in the back of her mind. It was a day Keisker would not forget and in an interview in 1970, she described that first meeting:

Elvis: 'If you know anyone that needs a singer ...'
Marion Keisker: 'What kind of singer are you?'
Elvis: 'I sing all kinds.'
MK: 'Who do you sound like?'
Elvis: 'I don't sound like nobody.'
MK: 'Do you sing hillbilly?'
Elvis: 'Yeah, I sing hillbilly.'
MK: 'Who do you sound like in hillbilly?'
Elvis: 'I don't sound like nobody.'

Elvis's natural ease with women must have stood him in good stead, though Keisker, a former Memphis radio presenter and scriptwriter, would have been vastly more sophisticated than the women Elvis was used to. He made a habit of dropping into the office regularly over the following months, ostensibly for a chat, but no doubt in the hope that he might be given a chance to sing. In the event, Keisker took a liking to the long-haired, still pimply six-footer with the killer cheekbones and shy manner, and would turn out to be quietly influential in getting his career off the ground.

Elvis had more than stars in his baby-blue eyes, though. Capricorns are hard workers, not layabouts, and he had no intention of giving up the day job to chase his dream. That summer, he left the machinist's shop and he and his cousin Gene went to work at the Precision Tool company, making munitions, where his Smith uncles, Travis and Johnny, were on the payroll. The two boys worked long hours and were well paid for it. Then Elvis, who must have harboured doubts about where his future might lie, or perhaps in a crisis of confidence not helped by the fact that his bosses were insisting he cut his hair, decided to think longer term. He found a job at Crown Electric, delivering electrical supplies by day and decided to study to become an electrician at night so that he would have a trade to fall back on. Every week, like the good son he was, he would hand over his wages to his parents, having taken out just enough for pocket money. He spent his spare time hanging around on the local Memphis music scene, cutting an oddball figure in his ballooning black pants with pink piping and bolero jackets from Lanskys. He must have been hoping that if nothing came of his Sun experience, he could perhaps get into a band. He had at least two auditions that winter, both unsuccessful – one with a gospel quartet he admired called the Songfellows – and must have been bitterly disappointed when he failed both. But life was far from uncomfortable materially that winter – by then, the Presleys had a television and a piano – but Elvis must have been itching and praying for some kind of break. Within a year, his prayers would be answered.

It all began with a second one-off disc he made at Sam Phillips's studio, four days before his nineteenth birthday in January 1954. This time Elvis sang 'Casual Love Affair' and 'I'll Never Stand In Your Way'. Afterwards, he met the man himself, who heard a quality in the teenager's voice that impressed him. If Phillips actually ever said, 'Don't call us, we'll call you', he meant it. Six months later, the phone rang. It was Marion Keisker. Could Elvis fill in on a demo session for a singer who hadn't turned up? Could he be there by three? He was half way through the door before he put the phone down. It is possible to imagine the sheer, breathtaking excitement he must have felt, the adrenaline surge that fuelled him as he tore down the road from the house on Alabama Street to meet his destiny.

As it turned out, the session didn't go quite as planned. Keisker had persuaded Phillips that Elvis might have the voice he needed for this job. Elvis sang all afternoon, every kind of song he knew, but Phillips wasn't thrilled. He could see Keisker's point – there was something about the boy. But what was it? He certainly didn't have 'hit' written all over him. Phillips decided Elvis needed 'a lot of work' and, with a view to developing whatever his talent might be, introduced him to Scotty Moore, a young guitarist who still had a day job but aspired to a career in music, and a bass player called Bill Black. A few jam sessions and a couple of weeks later, they were ready to record. Inside the hot studio on 5 July, Elvis was excited but extremely nervous – he may have felt that if he didn't come through this time, he wouldn't get another chance with Phillips. But the problem was that he hadn't yet found the right song – the catalyst that would release his own special sound. The song that would change his life – and everyone else's.

The session was flagging. There was no chemistry, nothing that smelled like a hit. Tired and fed up, they all took a break. Elvis, who always had to be drumming his fingers or strumming his strings, picked up the guitar. Just for fun, he began to clown about, singing a favourite number of his by the blues singer Arthur 'Big Boy' Crudup, mugging and playing for laughs. After a few minutes, Scotty and Bill joined in on guitar and bass, catching the infectious rhythm of the pace set by Elvis. On the other side of the glass, Sam Phillips's ears pricked up. He pressed the record button. It was his eureka moment – the sound and smell of a hit. The song was 'That's All Right (Mama)' and by behaving instinctively, being himself instead of trying to sing 'straight', Elvis had found his voice.

The birth of Elvis Presley as a recording star was a lucky accident. The chemistry created by the fusion of an old bluesy number sung by a young white boy with a voice like sex on legs, bottled by Sam Phillips that day, was pure gold. It would generate millions of dollars for years to come, long after its creator was dead and gone. And the record he cut that day – 'Blue Moon of Kentucky', a forties hit reworked in Elvis's idiosyncratic, rhythmic style would be the B-side – was the soon-to-be King's first hit, even if only in Memphis. It would soon sell 20,000 copies to a public hungry for the hot new sound of rock and roll and become a classic in the Elvis canon.

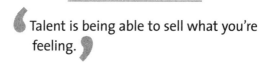

Talent is being able to sell what you're feeling.

Elvis went out that night with Dixie Locke, the girl he had been seeing since February, and his first serious love. She was only fifteen but they had already talked about getting married some day. Over soft drinks with Dixie, Elvis was casual about the day's achievement but, as the young singer sipped his milkshake, Sam Phillips's brain was whirring. He gave his friend Dewey Phillips, an influential DJ on the local WHBQ station's *Red, Hot and Blue Show*, a copy of 'That's All Right (Mama)'. Dewey (no relation to Sam) played it again and again that night, as many as fourteen times according to legend. The response was phenomenal – the switchboard was jammed with listeners ringing in to find out what the record was and where they could get a copy. Dewey wanted Elvis to appear live on the show that same night and rang the Presleys, but the budding star had gone off to see a film. Gladys, in a daze after hearing her son's name read out on the radio and the singing voice she knew so well, grabbed Vernon, and the pair trawled the cinema, taking an aisle each until they found Elvis and hauled him out to do his first interview with Dewey Phillips. What a night. Life would never be the same again.

Things began to happen fast. By the end of July, 'That's All Right (Mama)' had been released as a single, Elvis had appeared third on the bill on the prestigious *Slim Whitman Show* and he had signed his first management contract – with Scotty Moore, with whom he would have a long relationship, although he wouldn't last long as Elvis's manager.

On the back of this first single, Elvis, Scotty and Bill took to the road during the rest of 1954 and early 1955, touring small clubs and venues in Memphis and Texas, honing their sound and paying their dues. Along for the ride was Red West, the football star from LC Humes High who had stuck up for Elvis against the bullies and who was by now the first of the 'guys', not counting cousin Gene. By autumn 1954, Elvis was ready to fry some bigger fish, appearing on the legendary *Grand Ole Opry* in Nashville, where the performers were generally older and established; the conservative guardians of the country tradition didn't appreciate a youth they regarded as a hillbilly upstart. Elsewhere, though, he was going down a storm getting plenty of radio airplay and doing a regular slot on the *Louisiana Hayride* country showcase, in between one-night stands at venues all over the state and beyond, to Texas. Every night, like the good mama's boy he still was, he would take time out to ring home and reassure Gladys that he was all right.

Bob Neal, a Memphis DJ, manager and promoter who

had fingers in various entertainment pies, had heard Elvis on the *Hayride* and was struck by him. He would become the new manager, taking him on for 15 per cent commission. Scotty Moore wasn't fired – but as a musician still in his early twenties he wasn't equipped with the experience to take their careers further, and stood aside gracefully for the more experienced Neal.

Relatively speaking, this was the big time, but it wouldn't be long before Elvis would meet one of the most important people in his short life, the man who would make him a millionaire – Colonel Tom Parker. In the meantime, it was sheer hard graft for Elvis and the band, now calling themselves the Blue Moon Boys, but a darned sight more fun than driving a truck and learning about electrical circuits. Besides, their reputation was snowballing and Elvis's confidence was growing, boosted by his first television appearances, but mainly by the hysterical reaction of the audiences who were flocking to see him.

> The first time that I appeared on stage it scared me to death. I really didn't know what all the yelling was about. I didn't realize that my body was moving. It's a natural thing to me. So to the manager backstage, I said: "What'd I do?" And he said: "Whatever it is, go back and do it again".
> FROM AN MGM INTERVIEW, 1972

Word spread like wildfire as the band toured further afield – through Texas, Tennesssee, Arkansas, Missouri, Louisiana – and the public voted with their tonsils. Elvis might have had only a small repertoire but when he started jiggling his legs and curling his full-lipped baby mouth into a sensuous sneer, women went wild. He looked like nobody else, sounded like nobody else and moved like nobody else. When Elvis sang and gyrated on stage he unleashed a genie from a bottle and granted every female in the audience the wish fulfilment they had come for. One of his chief gifts was the ability to communicate via song; his words reached into hearts and minds and his body language spoke directly to their hormones. They were lost to this extraordinary persona – screaming and yelling, weeping and fainting. However, some of the men were less keen on the effect Elvis created. They liked the music but it was quite another thing to watch their wives and girlfriends under the influence of this strange-looking boy who flaunted his sexuality so blatantly on stage — they were jealous of this louche-looking alpha male who could whip up so much emotion. Red West usually went with Elvis, mainly to drive the car but also in case he needed protection. Little did those rednecks know that Elvis at this time was a God-fearing boy who was probably still a virgin, phoned his mama every day, drank nothing stronger than cola and kept a growing collection of teddy bears in his bedroom at home.

This touring phase was Elvis's apprenticeship – not only was he developing his act but he was learning how to exercise the sexual power he generated. He learned just how far he could push his audience. There may have been jealous rednecks ready to beat him up in the parking lots after his shows, but there were also girls who would have given anything for a brief, up-close and personal encounter with Elvis. For his part, he would always from this point on divide women into two groups: good girls and bad girls. And while he always treated the former with the respect and generosity he felt they deserved, he availed himself fully of the latter, though never regarded them as anything more than sex objects.

‘ Some people tap their feet, some people snap their fingers and some people sway back and forth. I just sorta do 'em all together, I guess. ’
1956

The image that had caused so many problems at school, and in some of his jobs, was now working in his favour. It might have provoked overt mockery on the streets – but it worked to perfection on stage where looking different was a plus. Still suffering from acne, he wasn't exactly handsome at the end of his second decade – in fact, his first publicity shot, probably taken in 1955, does him few favours. His still slightly pitted complexion is just discernible. The hair is razor-cut, shorter than usual and slicked back and up over sideburns that reach just past his earlobes. The eyes are dark, possibly enhanced with make-up, and the photograph captures neither the exquisite planes of his face nor the warmth of his personality. But that could be due to the fact that he is not smiling, and for good reason. He had a gap between his teeth that made him self-conscious. It wasn't until an orthodontist make him a cap after he began to make money that Elvis's famous smile would light up his public face.

> In public, I like real conservative clothes, something that's not too flashy. But on stage I like them as flashy as you can get them.

Under Bob Neal's promotion strategy, the money was rolling in and Elvis was making enough by 1955 to fulfil two of his dreams: he bought a pink Cadillac for himself and proudly moved Gladys and Vernon into a decent rented home – a modest two-bedroomed bungalow on Lamar Avenue, Memphis. At last things were looking up for the family. But bigger things still were on the horizon.

Thanks to the throngs that flocked to see him wherever he and the Blue Moon Boys played, Elvis had caught the eye of the self-styled 'Colonel' Tom Parker. The man who would catapult Elvis into the big league and make them both millions was an expert at the myth-making that is such a vital component of successful public relations. By the time he met Elvis, his greatest achievement to date was the construction of his own myth. He claimed to have been born in the West Virginia town of Huntington and to be an ex-military man. Despite his twenty-one stone frame, he did indeed have a military bearing and was fond of ordering people about. But he only ever served two years in the army, from 1929 to 1932 and some of it in the delightful environs of Hawaii – he was certainly never an officer. Perhaps the reality of army life didn't quite match up to the fantasy because, far from volunteering during the Second World War, he managed to avoid serving at all.

Besides, his thick Low Countries accent told another story about his origins. Tom Parker was actually born Andreas van Kuijk in Breda, Holland, on 26 June 1909, the fifth of nine children of a respectable working-class Catholic family. His father ran a stable, supplying working horses to the barge and freight companies that operated on the River Maas in the south. He was a wild child with a flair for making money, and obsessed with the circuses that occasionally passed through town. At eighteen, two years after the death of his father, he ran away – not to join a circus, but to America where he must have had some success because by the following year, he had saved enough money to visit his mother and siblings, bearing gifts and telling tales of how well the New World was treating him.

Back in the US, he enlisted and sent money home regularly to his mother, along with pictures of himself looking smart in army uniform. It was around this time that he changed his name. Perhaps like so many European immigrants, he had grown tired of having to spell out his name for people, or else he felt it would aid his assimilation in the English-speaking land of the free. There was no apparent need to gloss over his roots. But in 1932 his letters home dried up and the van Kuijks never heard from him again. His mother died in 1958, heartbroken, never knowing what had become of her adventurous, resourceful middle child, let alone that his was the business brain behind the King of rock and roll.

Before the Colonel – usually Colonel to Elvis, without the definite article, or the Admiral – got his hands on the goose that would lay so many golden eggs, he had had a colourful career, although many details remain murky, especially how he spent his time after leaving the army. It is known that he was employed in 1940 in Tampa, Florida, as chief dogcatcher and that he and his wife lived above the dog pound in a rent-free flat that went with the job. The edited highlights of Parker's life, according to his own version – now disproved – had him born into a Virginian family of carnival folk. As he told it, he was orphaned at the age of ten and joined his uncle's Great Parker Pony Circus. It is probably true that he worked in and around carnivals, travelling shows and circuses at various times, possibly after he came out of the army. But with his sharp eye for a main attraction, he branched out, swapping the sawdust and candyfloss of the fairground for showbiz in the mid-1940s. His biggest client before Elvis was Eddy Arnold, a country singer and later an actor who was most famous for his role in a television sitcom called *Green Acres*, which was shown during the 1960s in Britain.

The Colonel became almost a surrogate father to Elvis, who was soon his only client. He took care of business so that all Elvis had to do was make music and keep the money coming in. He was an old-looking forty-seven when he met the singer – tall, pudgy-faced and balding. The experienced promoter with his big talk and fancy cigar must have cut an impressive figure to an unsophisticated southern youth on his way up. And with his showman's nous, Parker recognized a money-spinner when he saw it. Elvis signed with the Colonel in March 1956. His new manager's paternalistic style meant that Elvis would miss opportunities in his personal as well as his professional life. If the Colonel didn't like a girlfriend, she would be eased out – Elvis generally complied with the Colonel's wishes. And he never toured abroad – the Colonel wouldn't allow it because he refused to leave the US himself. Elvis had always been extremely generous to good causes and had often performed benefits for charities but the colonel stopped him from doing anything free again, unless there was a way to make money through the back door. He wouldn't even be allowed to sing spontaneously or by prior arrangement for the troops when he was stationed in Germany during his military service.

And while the Colonel was indeed a King-maker, he was accused of stultifying Elvis's career once he came out of the army; as a man with dollar signs in his eyes, he couldn't see the point of paying royalties to first-class, internationally acclaimed songwriters such as Leiber and Stoller when tracks from Elvis's film soundtracks could be released as singles instead. That might have worked had the film songs always been great, but even Elvis's most ardent fans would admit that some of his movies were turkeys, and the songs did him few favours. Because of a deal the Colonel set up with song publishers Hill and Range, he effectively prevented Elvis from exploring new musical directions. The Colonel would have to ratify everything. Nor did he want Elvis to make films that would stretch him as the serious actor he dreamed of becoming; despite Elvis's undoubted potential, he was never allowed to fulfil it.

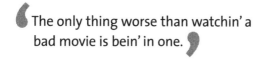

The only thing worse than watchin' a bad movie is bein' in one.

It is odd that Elvis rarely stood up to the Colonel in the early days, but he could be almost child-like in his acquiescence around the Svengali-like manager, who had a flair for manipulating people round to his way of thinking. And Elvis certainly had faith in the Colonel as a financial wizard – his management strategies launched Elvis's career beyond the small world of Dixie and made them both millions through record sales, film deals and merchandising. The Dutchman may have been a hard-gambling opportunist with an eye for a quick buck – he loved to spend copiously at the gaming tables – but he was also a genius in his own way. Although the Colonel has been described more than once as a classic con artist, he never ripped off the King behind his back. When he wanted money from Elvis, he was upfront about it – in 1967, he renewed his contract and negotiated his take all the way up to an audacious 50 per cent – a percentage worthy of a mobster. After Elvis's death, the Presley estate sued the Colonel, who had smartly tied up a deal with a grief-stricken Vernon in favour of his merchandising company, Boxcar Enterprises. A court ruled the deal unfair and a complex legal tangle ensued.

On 1 May, the day after his record 'Baby, Let's Play House' was released by Sun, Elvis and the Blue Moon Boys began their biggest tour yet – a month on the redneck trail as part of the Hank Snow All Star Jamboree, which also featured Bill Haley & the Comets and some big-name country acts. They had also added drummer DJ Fontana to the line-up to beef up their sound. Halfway through the tour, they found themselves on stage in front of their biggest audience ever – nearly 15,000 people – in Jacksonville, Florida; Elvis, resplendent in pink suit and lacy shirt, pulled out all the stops when it came to whipping the women and girls up into complete hysteria. Just audible over the screams at the end was a glistening, sweat-sodden Elvis thanking his audience; then, mouth almost eating the mike, with a wicked look in his eye and a come-on curl to his lip, he breathed: 'Girls, I'll see you backstage!' He was kidding, of course. But he wasn't to know that the girls had lost their sense of humour along with their equilibrium. Hundreds rushed the stage and then pinned him inside his dressing room. They wanted him and they wanted him now. He had to hide in a shower cubicle while security staff cleared the room. A terrified Elvis may have breathed a sigh of relief – only to discover when he finally escaped the building that his precious pink Cadillac was covered in lipstick graffiti and girls' names scratched into the paintwork. He was beginning to understand the unpredictable effect of the power he wielded on stage.

> ❛ Man, I was tame compared to what they do now. Are you kidding? I didn't do anything but just jiggle. ❜
> 1972

It was an intensive year of ever larger concerts, some of them booked by the Colonel who was working on his biggest gamble – wooing Elvis away from Bob Neal and on to a contract with himself, which was finally signed in August. He would get 25 per cent of takings, with Neal retained as adviser. But under the Colonel's wing, things were about to get even bigger. First, there was the Elvis Presley Jamboree tour in which he topped a bill that included Johnny Cash – in Lubbock, Texas, the supporting local act was a duo, one of whom was a young man with thick glasses and hair nearly as greased up as Elvis's – Buddy Holly.

❛Without Elvis, none of us could have made it.❜
BUDDY HOLLY

Then came the success that would catapult Elvis on to a much bigger stage. That September, Elvis had had three singles in the *Billboard* chart. It was as good as a calling card – within a couple of months the Colonel had negotiated a new, three-year record deal with RCA Victor, a major US label. It bought out his contract from Sam Phillips for $35,000 plus $5,000 for royalties owed to Elvis by the Memphis label. Just in time for Christmas, RCA released all four singles Elvis had made with Sam. But the company also wanted new material to capitalize on its new investment, and quickly – the sessions at the beginning of that year yielded a host of new songs, enough for a first album. They included 'Blue Suede Shoes', 'Tutti Frutti' and, arguably best of all, 'Heartbreak Hotel', which was immediately released as a single. It shot up the charts and sold a million copies by April, netting his first gold disc. Elvis was given a credit by the writer, Mae Axton, although he didn't contribute to either words or lyrics – a generous gesture on her part. It was a stunning song, inspired by a newspaper story about a suicide note, and a perfect launch pad for his first LP, simply titled *Elvis Presley*. A string of well-timed television appearances on *Stage Show*, which was broadcast nationally, helped to tempt the public palate and promoted Elvis, though he was forced to tone down his gyrations for the cameras.

The Colonel was making good on his promises. He might have been milking his client for all he was worth, but he seemed to be delivering the goods. At twenty-one, Elvis's dream was about to come true: he had spent hours imagining himself as his silver screen role models – James Dean, Marlon Brando and Tony Curtis. He was going to be a proper actor, just like the idols who had fed and sustained his *alter ego* for so long. Or so he hoped.

FAME AT LAST

His first screen test boded well. On April Fool's Day 1956, Elvis went to Hollywood and was recorded on celluloid at the Paramount studios singing 'Blue Suede Shoes' and acting a piece from *The Rainmaker*, the 1950s classic about a travelling snake-oil salesman, starring Burt Lancaster and Katharine Hepburn. He had done his homework and was word perfect. The same phenomenon that occurred every night on stage happened when the cameras began to roll – he may not have had technique but he could feel for his character, a love-struck southern youth. It was evident to producer Hal B Wallis, an A-list player with a formidable track record who went on to produce nine Elvis films, that this boy had that rare quality the camera loves – box office gold.

A Presley picture is the only sure thing in Hollywood.
HAL B. WALLIS

He and the Colonel struck a deal: Elvis would make three films for Paramount Pictures and receive $100,000 for the first, $150,000 for the second and $200,000 for the third. There was an option to extend his contract to seven years. For the next thirteen years, Elvis would have a relationship with Hollywood that mirrored the progress of a love affair, from the thrill of the initial encounter to the endgame of just going through the motions. He was never allowed to step too far beyond his own image, never to make a film in which singing wasn't required. He would move to Los

Angeles to make his movie debut in August but there was plenty to keep him busy before then.

He was touring – his first Las Vegas concert was a dismal failure; the casino crowd wasn't ready for what he had to offer, although he did meet and like Liberace, who shared Elvis's love of *outré* costumes – and recording, and because he was travelling greater distances, flying instead of driving. One night a plane he had chartered to take him and the Blue Moon Boys from Amarillo to Memphis got into trouble – the engine cut out. It turned out that there was barely enough fuel in the tank to get them to the landing strip. Another ten minutes and Elvis might have been lost to the world, like Buddy Holly, who died young in a plane crash. Elvis said at the time that he didn't know if he would ever fly again and kept flights to a minimum for the rest of his life, though he would own a private jet.

He was a national star, and if he needed further proof, *Life* magazine printed a story on him in its issue of 30 April. His face on the cover was enough to boost sales of any publication. He was swimming in money. He could indulge his love of cars and bikes, and acquired three Cadillacs and a Harley-Davidson motorcycle. And at last he bought the longed-for home for Gladys, putting down $40,000 in cash for a house at 1034 Audubon Drive, on a smart residential estate in Memphis, where the legions of fans who hung about outside drove the middle-class neighbours to distraction. The Presleys would live there for only a year but threw themselves into making 'improvements' to the low single-storey house, including putting in a swimming pool. It wasn't just the noise of the fans that upset the rest of the street but the continual sound of building work, indoors and out, not to mention the chickens Gladys kept in the back garden. Though for Gladys, now bereft of her boy for so much of the time, chickens were not enough to fill the gap in her life. She was suffering from empty-nest syndrome. Elvis's absences, despite his faithful phone calls, left her without the only role in life she wanted – to be his mama. Around this time, she turned to drink; for a woman who was also by now addicted to amphetamines in the form of diet pills which she had started taking in an effort to lose the excess weight that had piled on in middle age, these habits did not bode well for her health.

With three hits riding at Number One on the pop, R&B and country charts – 'I Want You, I Need You, I Love You'; 'Heartbreak Hotel' and 'I Forgot To Remember to Forget' – Elvis was the talk of the country. He was being likened to Frank Sinatra, who in his youth had inspired mobs of weeping, screaming fans. The smooth Sinatra was not enamoured of the comparison to Elvis.

Rock 'n' roll is the most brutal, ugly, degenerate, vicious form of expression – lewd, sly, in plain fact, dirty – a rancid-smelling aphrodisiac and the martial music of every side-burned delinquent on the face of the planet. FRANK SINATRA, 1956

Cynics might detect a touch of jealousy in a mainstream crooner a generation older who had also struggled to the top. However, Sinatra would one day eat his own words.

So who was Elvis at this point? Clearly he was no longer the virginal, insecure, pimply teenager in love with music and the idea of becoming a singer, but with no clear path ahead of him. In two short years, the hits, the money and the power it had given him to improve all three Presleys' lives had wrought big changes. Yet the trappings of fame hadn't gone to his head – that would happen later. He may not have been going to church every Sunday but he hadn't sold his soul to fame and Mammon. Instead of drinking and smoking off the adrenaline at the end of a night, he still liked to play and sing gospel songs and spirituals in the living room at Audubon Drive, where there were now four Cadillacs parked in the drive. At twenty-one, he was having a ball and already being hailed as the King of Rock and Roll.

> I ain't no saint but I've tried never to do anything that would hurt my family or offend God. I figure all any kid needs is hope and the feeling he or she belongs. If I could do or say anything that would give that kid that feeling, I would believe I had contributed something to the world.

It was a year since he had broken up with Dixie and although they were still in touch, he was now seeing June Juanico, a good-looking, sparky girl from Biloxi whom he had met on tour the previous year. Theirs was an apparently innocent relationship – she was one of the 'good girls' he enjoyed long relationships with, sometimes concurrently, and for years. They went out for spins on the Harley and Gladys welcomed her to the house, where she treated her like a daughter.

Big television engagements were lined up. He had made his first appearance on the *Milton Berle Show* in April, and a second on 5 June. Another top slot, the *Steve Allen Show* booked him for July but on one condition – he would not be allowed to corrupt the morals of viewers by doing the 'bump and grind' routine that had by now given him his rhyming nickname, 'The Pelvis'.

> I don't like to be called Elvis the Pelvis – it's one of the most childish expressions I've ever heard coming from an adult. But if they want to call me that, there's nothing I can do about it so I'll just have to accept it.

The producers surmounted the problem by having Elvis do an ultra-cheesy set. He sang his latest single, 'Hound Dog', to a live basset hound – it wasn't exactly rock and roll but viewers didn't care and the ratings were record-beating. Now the king of the TV variety shows called: it might well have been an honour to appear on the *Ed Sullivan Show* but Elvis wouldn't be doing it for the glory, and the Colonel negotiated a three-show contract which would net $50,000 – the most money ever paid to an entertainer on such a show. The Colonel had meant it when he said Elvis would never work for nothing, even when the programme was the best showcase in America for his new single.

'Hound Dog', with 'Don't Be Cruel' on the B-side, sold more than a million within three weeks of the first *Ed Sullivan* appearance. Before shooting started on his first film, Elvis went on tour. To the establishment, he represented all that was unholy, especially when they saw the King's effect on the cream of Florida's young maidenhood who returned from his concerts red-eyed, dishevelled and sighing with longing after being teased mercilessly from the stage. He was being denounced from pulpits across the country. A judge in Jacksonville, Florida actually went so far as to issue a warrant for Elvis's arrest, and although the Colonel smoothed things over, the star was told to dilute his routine as long as he remained in the state.

Elvis had been under the impression that his screen test meant that he would be acting in *The Rainmaker* with Lancaster and Hepburn. But it was not to be. When he moved out to Los Angeles to start shooting, it was to discover that *Love Me Tender* was a B-movie set in the civil war, selected to promote him as the next big thing, via the title song as well as his role. It was also to be made by 20th Century Fox because Hal Wallis had not found a script he thought right for his new talent. The film was a tale of love and revenge in which Confederate soldiers steal a Union payroll. The lead was played by Richard Egan, his younger brother by Elvis, and the female romantic interest in a tug

was enough to make Adams attractive to Elvis. His new pal would introduce him to the cream of young Hollywood, notably the legendary bad boy Dennis Hopper, and the exquisitely gamine Natalie Wood, then eighteen. To them, Elvis must have been a novelty: not only was he responsible for what was fast becoming the soundtrack of their lives, but he didn't smoke, drink or take drugs and was a Christian who believed his success was God-given. Adams stuck to Elvis like a limpet and Elvis was only too pleased – he took his friend home to Memphis and to Tupelo for the 1956 Memphis-Alabama Fair and Dairy Show. It was a true homecoming for the Tupelo boy made good. There was a near-riot during his performance and the show had to be stopped to calm the crowds.

Natalie Wood was also charmed, though perhaps not smitten, and when Elvis invited her and Adams home for a week to stay at Audubon Drive after the picture wrapped, they took up the invitation. They spent most of the first week of November exploring Elvis's turf in Memphis – and wherever he went, hundreds followed. Unlike the average tinsel-town celebrity, he didn't run and hide from the public but moved freely around the city, visiting old friends like Sam Phillips, eating in the cheap cafés that served the fatty southern dishes he adored, and giving dozens of autographs along the way. At Audubon Drive, there were hundreds of people camped outside, and Elvis did nothing to discourage them. It was like a fairground and just as noisy: there were fast-food vendors selling sustenance to hungry fans waiting for a glimpse of their idol. The gaggles of girls were even allowed to wander around the garden. It must have been an eye-opener for the visitors from Hollywood, who spent a bizarre few days cruising around with Elvis on motorbikes or in one of his growing fleet of cars and taking part in singalongs in the evenings along with Vernon and Gladys.

The golden days of that autumn, punctuated by his three ratings-beating appearances on the *Ed Sullivan Show*, saw not only the release of 'Love Me Tender' but also a series of wildly successful concerts in Texas. There were only two sour notes. The first was a notice from the draft board advising him that he was eligible for army service. The second was when he was famously provoked into a fight with a gas station manager in Memphis – Elvis had a temper and the older he got, the shorter his fuse became but in this instance it must have been hard to hold back. He had drawn up in the forecourt and, as usual, a big crowd formed round his brand new Lincoln when they saw who was driving. The manager, Edd Hopper, asked the star to move along. Elvis tried to explain that he couldn't start the car in case the fans got hurt. Hopper's response was to hit Elvis, who jumped out of the car and slugged Hopper back. A fight developed and the police were called; they charged both men and one of Hopper's employees with assault but Elvis was acquitted in court the next day. He was beginning to tot up the cost of fame: as well as being denounced on a weekly, if not daily, basis by the moral majority in the press and the pulpit for corrupting the youth of the nation with his act, there were more personal attacks. A month after the garage assault, a man who had been incensed to find that his wife kept a picture of Elvis in her purse tracked him down to his hotel in Toledo after a concert to start a fight with him, and ended up hitting Scotty Moore. Elvis jumped in to defend him and again the police were called. In yet another incident, one of his cars was trashed while it was parked outside a movie house. From now on, he would be more aware of his safety and start to gather round him the nucleus of the group later known as the Memphis Mafia: George Klein, Red West, Cliff Gleaves, Lamar Fike and his cousins Gene and Junior Smith.

By the end of 1956 Elvis had succeeded in notching up more songs in the *Billboard* Top 100 than any other artist since the chart began – his RCA sales amounted to more than twelve million. He had become a movie star, bought Gladys and Vernon a house and car, and enjoyed the company of a string of women. It had been a glorious twelve months and, if he had only known, perhaps the best of his life. For 1957 would be his mother's last year on Earth.

Elvis knew from the moment he got his draft notice that he would be going into the army. It was just a question of when and, whatever the Colonel might have thought, Elvis felt it was his duty to go. He had his medical on 4 January and got his classification notice along with his birthday mail four days later. He was A-1, more than fit to serve, and was told he would be called up in the second half of the year. In the meantime, there were more exciting things to think about: Hal Wallis had a film for him and there were new songs to record – the new soundtrack, and a store of potential singles and tracks for his first gospel album. And for the anti-Elvis brigade, there was a message from a man they might listen to: after his third and last appearance on *Ed Sullivan* on 6 January, the host announced to the nation: 'I wanted to say to Elvis Presley and the country that this is a real decent fine boy.'

For *Loving You*, his second film, Elvis dyed his dark blond hair black for the first time. He liked the look so much that he kept it for the rest of his life. Compared to *Love Me Tender*, the movie offered a superior story in a contemporary setting, a sparkling script and a much better role. His part, Deke Rivers, was a young up-and-coming singer looking for a break – easy enough for Elvis to relate to – and, of course, there was an angst-ridden love angle. Gladys and Vernon visited the Paramount set to watch their boy in action and were thrilled to be given parts by director Hal Kanter as extras in the audience during Deke's big concert scene; it must have been one of the great moments of Gladys's life, to be captured on celluloid sharing Deke/Elvis's triumph. After her death, Elvis would never watch the film again – seeing his mama's face lit up with such pride and happiness caused him too much pain. But *Loving You* would be a huge popular hit and 'Loving You/Teddy Bear' became Elvis's eighth million-selling single.

There are few buildings whose names are recognized the world over: Buckingham Palace, the White House, the Taj Mahal, the Louvre and, of course, Graceland. In March 1957, Elvis got an excited phone call from Gladys and Vernon. They had found a house a few miles south of Memphis that they thought he would like. They were right. When he went to view the eighteen-room colonial-style mansion, sitting in nearly twenty acres of grounds, it was love at first sight. He paid $100,000 – a vast amount in 1957 – not bothering to try to negotiate the price down because he wanted it so much. This was a palace fit for the King – or would be once he had completed a vastly expensive makeover that would turn the graceful house into a Las Vegas-style bachelor pad, complete with soda fountain, jukebox, eight-foot-square King-size bed, and peacocks on the lawn. Graceland was big enough to house as many of his family and expanding entourage as he liked. It would be his haven and, ultimately, his shrine. He spent as much time there as he could over the summer. Anita Wood, his new long-term girlfriend, was a frequent visitor. The 5ft 3in Wood, who Elvis nicknamed 'Little', would be a fixture in his life for five years, other women notwithstanding, and a loyal friend when he needed one.

> ❛Who is that fast-talking hillbilly son of a bitch that nobody can understand? One day he's singing to a dog, then to a car, then to a cow. They are all the same damn movie with that Southerner just singing to something different. ❜

Jailhouse Rock (MGM) was to be his most successful film to date, grossing $4 million, and would become a camp classic. It had a cracking soundtrack by two of pop's best songwriters, Jerry Leiber and Mike Stoller, who had written 'Hound Dog' and would also pen the score for *King Creole*. Again it was a story tailor-made for Elvis, about a truck driver convicted of manslaughter, who gets a chance to show what his golden voice can do in a prison talent contest. During filming that spring, he heard from an old acquaintance, unemployed former disc jockey Lamar Fike. Elvis invited Fike to his LA base in the penthouse at the posh Beverly Wilshire hotel and from the moment he arrived, the rotund, jolly Fike – perhaps the original Memphis Mafioso and certainly the first non-family member to join the household at Graceland – rarely left his side.

By autumn, Elvis knew his army service was just round the corner but there were recording sessions, mega-buck-generating sell-out concerts across the country – including a benefit in Tupelo in aid of a new youth centre – and another film to do first. In December, he got his notice to report for induction in the new year, on 20 January, but the army agreed to delay his conscription for two months so that he could make *King Creole*, thereby saving the studio from losing its investment in the production so far. Directed by the A-list Michael Curtiz for Paramount, and with Hal Wallis producing, there wasn't much different about the story (a young nightclub singer gets into a fight over a woman but redeems himself with his golden voice). However, it was a good script and, guided by Curtiz, Elvis put in a sterling performance – even the critics liked it, though the film did less well at the box office than *Jailhouse Rock*. Notably, it co-starred Walter Matthau.

Back in Memphis and ready to swap his slick, dark quiff and sideburns for the mandatory crew-cut, Elvis threw the mother of all leaving parties – a ten-night extravaganza at the Rainbow Rollerdome. On 24 March, surrounded by his entourage including the Colonel and his parents, Private Elvis Aron Presley, number 55310761, was sworn in and departed by bus with the other fourteen recruits for Fort Chaffee in Arkansas, to undergo basic training. On arrival they were greeted by a carnival atmosphere. Fans lined the route to the base and, mindful of public relations, the army allowed the press corps full access to its celebrity recruit, and the cameras recorded the now famous photographs of his crowning glory being shorn to the bone. He was issued with his pressed khakis and transferred to Fort Hood, Texas, where he would sleep on a bunk and learn to shine his boots and clean his rifle. Private Presley, Company A, 2nd Medium Tank Battalion, 37th Armour, 2nd Armoured Division, would become one of the rank and file. For eight weeks, that is; after basic training he was permitted to live off-base and rented a comfortable house in nearby Killeen for himself, his parents, grandmother and Fike; the place was always full of visitors, including Anita Wood, and became a home from home.

While Elvis was out of commission, and the fans were besieging the army with calls and letters for their idol, the Colonel was keeping the business machine ticking over, as he would during the singer's entire two-year army stint.

He didn't want his boy to be forgotten just because he was serving his country overseas. Not that there was much danger of that.

> I've eaten things in the army that I never ate before and I've eaten things that I didn't know what it was, but after a hard day of basic training you could eat a rattlesnake.

The senior Presleys had never been abroad, but the plan was that they would join Elvis once his unit was posted to Germany later in the year, although Gladys was terrified by the prospect of living in a strange country. Then something occurred that no one had foreseen or imagined. Gladys began to complain of feeling ill. Nothing eased her discomfort and intense nausea, and on 8 August she and Vernon left Texas for Memphis, so that she could consult her own doctor. He arranged for her to be admitted to hospital immediately; her startling yellow hue indicated jaundice but the diagnosis was uncertain. Almost as soon as she was hospitalized, Gladys began to go downhill and Elvis, who had been making frantic phone calls to her doctors, applied for compassionate leave. The army denied it, until Elvis threatened to go AWOL and Gladys's doctor (ex-army himself) put pressure on Elvis's commanding officer to let him go. When the King eventually reached his mother's bedside she was extremely ill. He and Vernon kept a bedside vigil over the next thirty-six hours and then

Gladys appeared to perk up slightly. Elvis was persuaded that it was safe to go home – he went to the cinema, then back to Graceland. Just after 3 am on 14 August, Vernon rang the house. Gladys was dead. Elvis's mama, his 'best girl' had gone for ever.

> It wasn't only like losing a mother, it was like losing a friend, a companion, someone to talk to. I could wake her up any hour of the night if I was worried or troubled about something.

Beside himself, Elvis rushed to the hospital. In grief, he reverted to the baby language of his youth, talking to his mama, wailing and keening like the mountain people he had come from. 'Satnin' is gone, my baby is gone,' he would cry to anyone who would listen. He touched her and stroked her 'itty bitty sooties' and her 'itty bitty ears' until the staff had to ask him to stop. Gladys's body was taken back to Graceland for the wake but had to be removed to an undertaker's when half the town turned up and camped out in the grounds. His friend Nick Adams and Anita Wood rushed to his side. Even Dixie Locke arrived to support him in his lonely hour of need.

There was never an autopsy but it was concluded that Gladys had died of a heart attack, and perhaps complications involving the liver and her digestion. And maybe the actual cause of death didn't matter much to

Elvis: all that mattered was that she had gone, and at the relatively young age of forty-six. He would never be the same – nothing would ever quite salve his pain. Gladys was at peace but her son was trapped in a torment of grief.

KING AND COUNTRY

It was John Lennon who said that Elvis died the day he went into the army. Lennon was talking about the music but there was another dimension to his remark. A part of Elvis had died with his mother. From his arrival in Germany, his behaviour would begin to change, and not for the better. The main reason was that Elvis discovered drugs in the army and began to consume amphetamines. Although he would eventually become addicted to prescription drugs, he never regarded his own habit as such: in the 1960s, he would loathe the illegal drugs of the counter-culture and volunteer his services to President Richard Nixon as a federal narcotics agent. In this respect, Elvis suffered from a bad case of chronic denial.

He also began to smoke the small cigars he would from now on enjoy in private, though never in public. Although that can hardly be described as drug abuse, the old Elvis would never have lit up, and while alcohol would never be a part of his life, his days of clear-headed abstinence were about to end.

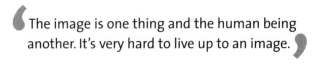

The image is one thing and the human being another. It's very hard to live up to an image.

In late September 1958, he boarded the *USS Randall* for the week-long voyage to the naval port of Bremerhaven to find a mob of hysterical fans and a vast press contingent gathered to meet the ship on 1 October. His unit, the 32nd Tank Battalion, Third Armoured Division, was based at Friedberg, headquarters of the US 7th Army, where Private Presley was assigned at first to drive a jeep for his lieutenant-colonel. A week after his arrival, Vernon, Minnie Mae, Red West and Lamar Fike joined him in Germany. Elvis missed Memphis but at least he had his own household around him. After he got permission to move off base, the entourage took over the whole top floor of the Hotel Gruenwald in Bad Nauheim, a cobbled and turreted spa town a few miles from the base. Elvis might have to scrub out the latrines and shine his boots with the rest of the troops, but at least he could relax among his family and friends. And to lessen his homesickness, a month after his arrival, who should be topping the bill at a concert in Stuttgart but Bill Haley & the Comets. Elvis couldn't pass up the chance to go and watch his old friend perform and to renew the acquaintance afterwards. There were other distractions. He had bought his first German car – a BMW sports model. He had also been dating a sixteen-year-old typist called Margit Buergin, described in his letters home to various friends as his 'little German chuckaloid', but he soon met another girl who would become a fixture in his life until after he returned home to the US. Elisabeth Stefaniak was only looking for an autograph but got a lot more than that. Elvis took a liking to the pretty American whose stepfather was a sergeant stationed over there, and they began to go out almost every night. After his field training was over, he invited her to become his secretary –

her fluency in German would be an asset – which would be a live-in position at the Hotel Gruenwald. There was plenty of fan mail to answer, after all, but he didn't tell her at that stage that her duties would include sharing a bed with the boss. It must have been an odd experience for a nineteen-year-old army brat to go from a strict home to the hotch-potch Presley household in which the only other female was Elvis's grandmother. She had been instructed not to talk to any of the men in the house bar her employer. Naturally, Elisabeth was utterly starstruck and could not believe her luck.

> ‘I've had a pretty good lesson in human nature. It's more important to try to surround yourself with people who can give you a little happiness because you can only pass through this life once, Jack. You don't come back for an encore. ’

But the hotel management had just about had enough: they might have been paying their bills on time but the Presley entourage had overstayed its welcome. Not only did Red and Lamar like to play with water pistols and shaving foam, they managed to set one of the rooms on fire. Elvis decided to do what he should have done in the first place – rent a house where they could live and eat as they chose. Minnie Mae would at last have a proper role to play, housekeeping and cooking the southern food they all loved. And there would be plenty of room for Elisabeth, too, in the substantial three-storey house that was Goethestrasse 14, Bad Nauheim. Although the traditional, old-fashioned decoration and furnishings were not to his taste (how he must have longed for the plush modernity of Graceland) the house would function as a home-from-home: just as they did in Memphis, the fans would faithfully line up outside and Elvis would go out and sign autographs every night. Meals were taken *en famille*, the reassuring down-home flavours that took the edge off his homesickness. Minnie Mae prepared all the things they liked – tinned hot dogs, peanut butter and luncheon meat could be bought on the base. And they had also discovered that German food was not so very different from what they were used to in Memphis. Elvis had always loved sauerkraut, pork and mashed potatoes.

But what sort of soldier was Elvis? Instead of playing the star and shirking his duties, which he could have done, he threw himself into becoming as professional a soldier as he could. He had never been lazy – he had worked hard since the various after-school jobs of his youth. His attitude stood him in good stead and he adapted easily to the routine and repetition of military life. It was just as well – anything less than a wholehearted performance would have given his critics ammunition. For he was being watched. Unlike his fellow recruits, Elvis was never going to be able to slot in easily as just one of the guys. He had something to prove. Again his hardworking, modest attitude reaped rewards, just as it had in Hollywood. Not only was he accepted and respected by his peers but he was promoted to Private 1st Class after the unit got back from field training two months after his arrival – he would eventually return to the US with his sergeant's stripes.

Elvis loved being a tank gunner – he had a lifelong obsession with guns of all kinds – but the assignment wasn't good for him; as a child he had suffered from ear infections which may have left his hearing vulnerable, and the phenomenal noise created by the big shells used in training began to have an effect. It was Lamar who spotted it. He though Elvis was ignoring him one day when he didn't respond to a question about how the day had gone. Elvis just hadn't heard because his ears were ringing. Lamar told the Colonel, who pulled strings at the Pentagon to have his boy moved off the tanks. In middle age Elvis would become increasingly hard of hearing and his army experience may have contributed to this.

Elvis had Lamar and Red, but his best army buddies were Charlie Hodge, a musician he had met *en route* to Germany, and Rex Mansfield. Elvis loved to confer nicknames and soon christened the latter 'Rexadus' – the name would stick, as would Rex, who fitted right into his tight little group with Lamar and Red. Later, he would make another long-term army friend, Joe Esposito, who would join the Memphis Mafia but who also had connections to the real Mafia.

With his new home, family, friends, Elisabeth and a never-ending supply of willing girls flitting in and out of his bedroom, plus regular chats with the Colonel and Anita back home, Elvis settled down. After all, Germany was only for a little while, a blip in the Colonel's grand scheme

– the big publicity build-up to his return home would commence in just a few months.

If Elvis was feeling pretty good around this time, it wasn't just because he had found stability. He was on a chemical high. As far as he was concerned, Dexedrine was a miracle drug; he had been introduced to it by someone on the base and had a ready source of supply. Elvis didn't consider these drugs to be dangerous or even illegal, despite the fact that he was buying them under the counter and paying black market rates. After all, they were only diet pills and everyone took them. They were great for keeping the weight down and it was just a bonus that they gave you such an energy boost – you could even magnify the effect if you drank plenty of strong coffee. And as anyone who has ever taken drugs knows, there's no fun in doing it alone: soon he was handing them out to the guys too. They were especially useful when Elvis was on leave and he and the boys could take trips to Munich and Paris, say, to let off steam and have fun with showgirls — those handy little pills meant they never had to sleep at all.

But what goes up must come down – whether or not Elvis made the connection is impossible to know but around this time he began to experience mood swings. There were small cruelties; always jealous, he became suspicious that his friends were not as loyal as they should have been. He kept a close eye on Elisabeth to make sure she wasn't breaking his rules about talking to Red and Lamar, let alone other men. One example that illustrates his unreasonable behaviour took place in January of 1959. Vernon and Elisabeth were in a serious car crash on the

Autobahn. He was driving the BMW, which was reduced to a write-off, she was in the passenger seat. Although Vernon was fine apart from shock, Elisabeth was rushed to hospital with a suspected broken back. As she recovered, the man who would have a hit with 'Suspicious Minds' a decade later grilled the girl whose bed he shared about what she had been doing to cause Vernon to lose control of the wheel – he was convinced they were having an affair.

This sort of behaviour could be attributed to the effect of Gladys's death but it is much more likely that it was caused by the Dexedrine. It is now acknowledged that the appetite suppressants prescribed in the late 1950s and 1960s were not, in fact, harmless but led in some people to addiction and behavioural problems – and Elvis was not taking measured prescription doses. He stocked up on huge jars of the pills and just popped them when he felt like it. No doubt they also numbed the pain he felt at the loss of Gladys but it is likely that the way in which his personality – not to mention his ego – developed over the next decade owed something to his heavy amphetamine use from this point onwards.

Then something happened to really upset him. Vernon began seeing a woman. His father might have been only forty-two, but Gladys had been in the grave just a few months, and Elvis was appalled. He saw his father's willingness even to consider a new relationship at this point as an insult to his mother's memory. He was still in mourning and felt deeply disturbed that his father was ready to move on. Dee Stanley was in her early thirties and married to an older sergeant on the base, who had served in both the Korean and Second World Wars. Eventually Dee would leave her husband for Vernon and join him in Memphis with her three young sons, Billy, Rick and David. Elvis must have wanted Vernon to be happy but he would never fully embrace the woman he felt had usurped his mother's place and he did not attend the wedding in Alabama, in July 1960.

By the middle of 1959, the Colonel was on the offensive. Some of Elvis's pre-recorded material was released to remind the fans, as if they had forgotten, that Elvis would be back soon. There was no need to worry. 'A Big Hunk O' Love' would spend fourteen weeks in the chart that summer, reaching Number One. A second single, 'My Wish Come True', made it to Number Twelve and RCA also released an album, *A Date With Elvis*, featuring the King in uniform on the cover. There was more news from home: there was a movie project in the pipeline that would make a story out of Elvis's spell stationed in Germany – *GI Blues*.

Then, four months before Elvis's discharge, something happened to change the course of his future. He met Priscilla. In many ways, she was his ideal. At fourteen, Priscilla Anne Beaulieu was ten years his junior – a petite and impressionable teenager with a face like an angel. A well-brought-up, middle-class girl, her father was a US Air Force captain stationed at Wiesbaden. Unlike many of Elvis's other girls – the groupies and autograph hunters – she didn't go looking for him. Currie Grant, an airman friend of Elvis's, had seen her in a café whiling away the day with her brother and asked if she would like to meet him. It is hard to imagine that he didn't know what kind of reaction a visit from this sweet, exquisite girl would provoke in the King. Naturally, she begged her parents to let her go to the house on Goethestrasse at the weekend with Grant and his wife. From the moment Elvis saw her arrive through the door of his living room, he was smitten. Not only was Priscilla a budding beauty, she was not overwhelmed by his star status. She was an intelligent, self-confident girl who could make conversation. She may not have known what she was getting into, but she was a sympathetic, empathetic person. Soon, despite the fact that she was still at school, Elvis wanted to see her several times a week. Her parents took a great deal of persuading, but eventually caved in after Elvis went to see them. Elvis and Priscilla spent those evenings in his bedroom and he made her his confidante – the confused inner boy who was bereft of his beloved mother reached out to this American girl who knew how to listen and was so beautiful to behold. Priscilla was different, he knew that – there was a connection with her that he had never experienced before. It is possible that he was already thinking about marrying her, although back in Memphis, Anita Wood was under the impression that she was still the one. He was still exchanging letters and phone calls with Anita, and Elisabeth was still his human hot water bottle – he never had sex with Elisabeth, who was a 'good girl', although they always slept together. For Elisabeth, the novelty of life with the King had palled – she and Rex Mansfield began to see each other in secret, terrified that Elvis would find out. Although she would return to the US to work for Elvis, she and Rex married soon afterwards. Elvis did not attend.

The newlyweds found themselves banished from the Kingdom.

Christmas that year was the best Elvis had had for a couple of years and, in his happy mood, he gave a big party for friends and family. He was looking forward to leaving for home in three months but the main reason for his good mood, of course, was Priscilla whose gift from him was a solid gold and diamond watch. Anita's confidence in her position in Elvis's life must have taken a beating when she saw a widely circulated press photograph of Priscilla waving a tearful farewell to the King on his way back to the US, not to mention the caption that went with it in which Priscilla was described as his German girlfriend.

As he prepared to leave for home, Elvis was promoted to sergeant and put in charge of a reconnaissance unit – he had done well in the army, never exploiting his celebrity and gaining his stripes on merit alone. He could be proud of himself. In March, he boarded a military plane and flew home to a hero's welcome.

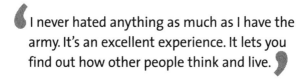

I never hated anything as much as I have the army. It's an excellent experience. It lets you find out how other people think and live.

CAUGHT IN A TRAP

The 1960s was a difficult decade for Elvis. He had heralded the extraordinary creative explosion in rock and pop that had produced and influenced many of its most exciting talents, including the Beatles, the Beach Boys and Phil Spector. But for much of the time, he himself was held back from exploring different avenues in music and on film by Colonel Tom Parker. While the artists who would create the sounds of the 60s were innovating almost by the week, the Colonel made sure Elvis slipped into the mainstream. While London was swinging, and young Californians were dreaming of peace and love at Big Sur, glitzy Las Vegas became Elvis's second home. And while his personal spiritual search acquired fresh urgency, his essential conservatism, hatred of illegal drugs – despite his own escalating consumption of prescription pills – and love of guns meant that for much of the time he was culturally out of step with the times.

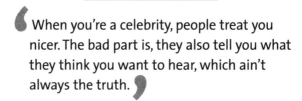

‘ When you're a celebrity, people treat you nicer. The bad part is, they also tell you what they think you want to hear, which ain't always the truth. ’

Home from the army, Elvis settled back down to work. He had not been forgotten by the fans and to capitalize on the hoopla surrounding his return, MGM re-released *Jailhouse Rock*. Elvis headed for Nashville to record the first in a series of productive sessions that would yield several hits, including 'Stuck On You', 'It's Now Or Never' and 'Are You Lonesome Tonight?', before beginning a tour of the southern states, the highlight of which was a pre-recorded slot on the *Frank Sinatra Show*, in which the two tuxedoed titans duetted on 'Witchcraft' and 'Love Me Tender'. He was back in business, on top of the world.

The Colonel had a gruelling schedule lined up for his boy – in 1960, Elvis made three films: *GI Blues*, *Flaming Star* and *Wild In The Country*. Usually he and the guys stayed at the Beverly Wilshire hotel but the management had grown tired of their rowdy behaviour and asked them to leave. Besides, it made more sense to rent a house. Elvis was always more comfortable in a place where he could spread out and install a jukebox, and they moved into plush quarters suitable for rock and roll royalty at 565 Perugia Way in Bel Air – the house was previously owned by the Shah of Iran. Set on a hill, this would become the scene of legendary, almost nightly, parties. Unlike other Tinseltown *soirées*, they were all-women affairs. Apart from Elvis and the guys, of course. The rule was that Elvis had *droit de seigneur* – first pick of the girls. Hundreds of cute Hollywood wannabes, chosen specifically to conform to Elvis's ideal type, passed through the front door in the hope of entertaining the King.

If he were partying like there was no tomorrow, at least he wasn't drinking – others could down whatever they liked but Elvis stuck to cola. He had left the army fit, and to stay in shape and keep his weight down, he maintained the obsessive interest in karate sparked during his basic training and continued in Germany – he was so proficient that after two years he had a First Dan black belt. He also developed a passion for waterskiing and bought a boat, which he christened *Karate*.

Elvis loved animals, especially horses and dogs, and always had a menagerie of pets. He also liked monkeys and apes. Michael Jackson would one day become famous for his pet chimpanzee, Bubbles, but Elvis got there first. He bought Scatter as a mature chimp with a taste for alcohol, who had been taught how to drive. The animal would be dressed up like a little man in a suit and tennis shoes, and let loose at the film studios to terrify unsuspecting executives and secretaries. Even more fun for Elvis was to let Scatter roam the Bel Air house during a party: the chimp would get drunk and then embark on his favourite pursuit – lifting and looking up women's skirts, after which he would indulge in the lewd behaviour that comes naturally to apes.

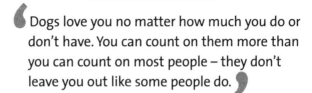

Dogs love you no matter how much you do or don't have. You can count on them more than you can count on most people – they don't leave you out like some people do.

Paramount's *GI Blues*, while no stretch in acting terms, was a massive popular hit, as was the album which reached Number One in the charts. Both *Flaming Star* and *Wild In The Country*, which were made by 20th Century Fox, appeared to promise Elvis more than they delivered: good writers (playwright Clifford Odets scripted the latter) and marginally less formulaic roles. However, Elvis did not have the training to make much of his parts. He had always refused to consider acting lessons, and now his lack of technique was beginning to show.

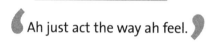

Ah just act the way ah feel.

If he had previously managed to put up creditable performances by 'feeling' his way into the parts, it no longer worked. It should have – he was riding high on a wave of popularity and looked better than ever, thanks to his karate workouts, and these two films were potential opportunities to develop his limited acting experience into something more. So why couldn't he rise to the challenge? The most likely explanation is that he was more or less constantly medicated on amphetamines and the sleeping pills he needed to get to sleep. The uppers gave him energy and lowered his appetite, but the drugs dimmed what natural acting talent he possessed, and possibly dulled his ability to 'feel' anything much at all as far as his characters were concerned, let alone project convincingly.

His thespian shortcomings would matter much less in his next film, which would be his biggest hit – *Blue Hawaii*. Produced by Hal Wallis for Paramount, and the first in a newly negotiated five-film deal worth $825,000 in total, it was a jolly musical comedy set in the Pacific paradise and packed with romantic songs – 'Can't Help Falling In Love', would be his twenty-ninth gold disc – and sunny aloha magic: on release it would gross $14m and set and seal the formula for the pictures he would make for the rest of his career. (At that time the Colonel also struck an even more lucrative deal with MGM: $2 million for four pictures plus 50 per cent of profits.) Elvis could not complain about the money, but the dream of joining James Dean and Marlon Brando in the silver-screen pantheon was well and truly over. Before filming began, he gave a benefit concert in Honolulu to raise funds for the memorial to commemorate the *USS Arizona*, which was sunk with all hands on deck in the bombing of Pearl Harbor and preserved as a living tomb.

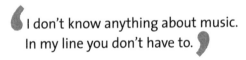

' I don't know anything about music. In my line you don't have to. '

In tandem with his ongoing relationship with Anita Wood, in Hollywood he had been seeing the teenage Tuesday Weld, his co-star in *Wild In The Country*, and a wardrobe assistant from Fox. If Anita knew about and was willing to put up with his compulsive womanising, whether he slept with them or not (and he never slept with his 'good girls'), something was about to happen that would change how she felt about their future together. Elvis invited Priscilla to visit. Despite the parade of party girls in LA, no one compared to the teenage dream he remembered from so many happy evenings at Bad Nauheim: only Priscilla really understood him. From his perspective, this would be a slow-burning relationship – he already wanted to marry her but was happy to wait until she was over twenty-one. Besides, it suited his *modus operandi* to wait – once the relationship was consummated, he would lose interest, as he always did.

It wasn't easy to get Priscilla's parents' permission; she was still only sixteen. But after persistent pressure and persuasion, they agreed to let their daughter visit for two weeks on various conditions, one being that she stay with a family of Elvis's acquaintance and not under his roof. In fact, after a guided tour of Hollywood and its delights, he whisked her off to Las Vegas, by now his favourite spot for rest and relaxation. If she had envisaged a fortnight of quality time *à deux,* Priscilla got a rude awakening. They drove to the casino capital in Elvis's brand-new customized motor home – a sixteen-year-old girl, the King of Rock and Roll and, of course, several of Elvis's guys. But once ensconced in a luxury suite at a top hotel in the neon and plastic heaven/hell that is Las Vegas, things began to look up. Time and attention were lavished on Priscilla who was given a sophisticated makeover: big hair, smoky eyes and an immaculate wardrobe fit for a King's consort.

Her visit just whetted Elvis's appetite. He invited Priscilla to Graceland at Christmas, for him probably the happiest festive season he had spent since his mother's death – her gift from him was a diamond ring. Elvis suggested that she spend her last year of schooling in Memphis so that they could be near each other. Over the next few months, Priscilla's parents were gradually persuaded to let their daughter go. She would live with Vernon and Dee in their house on the edge of the property, although in practice she soon moved into Graceland, driving herself to school in the little red sports car Elvis bought her. Although he undoubtedly loved her, it would be five years before they married.

Politically, the early 1960s was a curious mixture of optimism and fear in America. The Cold War was at its chilliest; for a short while the world held its breath over the Bay of Pigs crisis and worried about whether they had enough sandbags in case the Communists attacked. But John F Kennedy and Jackie reigned in the White House and much of America believed in the promise of better things to come. Then, in November 1963, the golden hope of democratic America was shot and killed by Lee Harvey Oswald as JFK's motorcade cruised through Dallas, sending shockwaves reverberating across the world. It was the catalyst for an unsettled era that would usher in a new kind of music and a grassroots political movement, as the United States moved further to the right and became embroiled in Vietnam. The times were a-changing across the Atlantic too, especially in London and Liverpool. In February 1964, the Beatles made their US television début on the *Ed Sullivan Show*. The public went berserk. Nothing like it had been seen before – at least not since Elvis's pre-army heyday. Suddenly rock and roll was dead, or at the very least comatose. Rock had arrived. Although he still had a loyal fan base and his records continued to sell well, Elvis had lost his edge. He was only twenty-nine, but the Beatles were younger and fresher, and making a sound that was right for the times. Elvis hadn't performed on stage in front of a live audience for years; he was churning out mediocre movies, hanging out in Las Vegas and Hollywood and getting himself appointed an honorary sheriff of Shelby County, Tennessee. Compared to the Beatles, it wasn't very rock and roll.

He was moody, worrying about the storm the new Liverpool group were causing. But, in fact, he need not have been concerned – not yet thirty, he was still the undisputed King.

❝I doubt very much whether the Beatles would have happened if it was not for Elvis. God bless you, Elvis.❞
PAUL McCARTNEY

How Elvis must have hated what he had become – if he allowed himself to feel anything much at all. His favourite book was now the *Physician's Desk Reference*, *PDR* for short. It was his bible. He grew adept at creating combinations of various uppers and downers in the doses he needed to control his body clock on artificial twenty-four-hour time, partying late and sleeping the daylight away. He would also dispense them to various members of his entourage, and voiced to at least one interviewer the thought that he would like to have been a doctor, although pharmaceuticals were more accurately his field of study.

This was a time when Elvis began to examine the way he was leading his life. He returned to the old question of why God had chosen to give this special talent to him. He was hungry for something, but not sure what. Interestingly, his search didn't lead him to the evangelistic churches of his youth. But in April 1964, someone arrived, literally, on his doorstep to point the way forward. Larry Geller was a hairdresser, a replacement for Elvis's usual man. But Geller was no ordinary stylist. Their small talk during the snipping and spraying routine took an unexpected turn into philosophical territory. Like Elvis, Geller believed himself to be a serious seeker after truth, but the fact that he was about four years further along the path made him indispensable to the King at this stage. Geller put together a reading list for his celebrity client: Yogananda's *Autobiography of a Yogi*, Krishnamurti's *The First and Last Freedom*, *The Tibetan Book of the Dead*, Madame Blavatsky's *The Secret Doctrine* and *The Voice of Silence*, even the *Bible*. Elvis devoured them all and asked for more; he delved into numerology, Judaism, astrology and philosophy. These volumes were mostly dotty spiritual handbooks that would be similarly embraced by the wackier fringes of the Woodstock generation. Where a hippie might have dropped acid and stayed up all night reading the *Tibetan Book of the Dead*, Elvis took a handful of Dexedrine to enable him to study through the small hours. In the middle of this voyage into the unknown, he took a break to make a record: not another superficial, poppy soundtrack, but a gospel album – *How Great Thou Art* – that brought him his first Grammy award, for the best spiritual album of the year.

Elvis confided in Geller that he talked to his lost twin, Jesse Garon, that he could hear his brother's voice inside his head. He also talked to Gladys. When Geller didn't laugh, it must have been a huge relief for him – who else in his circle would have understood? Not Red, Lamar, or the other guys. In fact, most of them heartily disliked Geller, who actually moved into the household for a while with his wife and family. And Priscilla certainly didn't welcome his presence. In this respect, she was not on the King's wavelength.

> I've seen a UFO, never any ghosts. But I believe in an afterlife so it's possible. When I'm home, I can feel my mama's presence.

To Priscilla and the rest of Elvis's gang, Geller was a cuckoo in the nest and what made it worse was that they had to listen to Elvis spouting his crazy theories and demonstrating the telekinetic powers he believed he possessed. He was regularly visiting an ashram run by disciples of Yogananda in the Hollywood Hills, and commissioned a landscaped meditation garden for

Graceland, where he could spend time in contemplation.

More disturbingly, Elvis also began to have visions, on one occasion seeing Stalin's face in the clouds metamorphose into Christ's face. Always superstitious, he thought numbers were imbued with significance. The guys mocked Geller, blaming him for the change in Elvis's behaviour and calling him the Swami, Rasputin, and worse, behind his back. But as well as exasperation, they must have felt afraid for Elvis who had now swapped sex for death as his chief leisure interest, even visiting undertakers to look at cadavers. His old friends wanted him back on planet Earth. Fortunately for them, so did the Colonel, who was not pleased that someone else exerted a level of influence that threatened his own. After three years, Geller's days as *de facto* spiritual adviser to the King were numbered, although he and Elvis remained friends until the end.

In 1965, the year he turned thirty, Elvis beat the Beatles to the top of the British charts with 'Crying In The Chapel' and the Fab Four finally got to meet the man who had first inspired them, visiting him one night in LA. Their time had come, but the King still ruled the world – his earnings for the year were estimated at $5.5 million, making him the highest-paid entertainer on the planet.

> When you let your head get too big, it'll break your neck.

Elvis and Priscilla chose Christmas 1966 to announce their engagement, a diamond ring sparkling on her left hand. However, they wouldn't marry for a further eighteen months and, in the meantime, Elvis began a cycle of binge-eating and crash-dieting. He had never refined his palate. The only foods he enjoyed were the starchy, sugary, fatty dishes of his childhood. The only fruit and vegetables he would consume were sliced tomatoes, sauerkraut and bananas which, together with peanut butter and jam or 'jelly', formed his favourite sandwich filling. Added to his drug consumption, which not only affected his metabolism but leeched vitamins and minerals from his system, this was a diet destined to lead to tragedy. It is possible that the extreme bloating and digestive problems he suffered from as he got older were due to an imbalance in his digestive flora, perhaps exacerbated by antibiotics – his symptoms were consistent with *candida* overgrowth in the gut. Crash-dieting also weakened his system, as did the laxatives and diuretic salt tablets he took to shed poundage quickly so that he was fit to work in front of the camera. And the Colonel did keep him working: in 1967, the King signed a new ten-year deal with his manager, giving Parker 50 per cent of all profits.

As befits a seeker of truth, Elvis gave some of his fortune away to good causes; he had always been generous but now the amounts were larger. He donated some money to the ashram, but Memphis charities benefited most. He also went on a huge shopping spree: seventeen horses – one each for his family and closest friends – which were stabled at Graceland and exercised daily in the grounds. Then he bought the Circle G, a working ranch, across the border in Mississippi – he had a notion it might work as a commune, though that would never happen – and a Learjet.

'Sometimes when I walk into a room at home and see all the gold records hanging on the walls, I think they must belong to another person, not me. I just can't believe that it's true. '

When Elvis and Priscilla finally married on 1 May 1967, it was not the big showbiz wedding expected of rock and roll royalty. Nor was there any kind of spiritual element to the ceremony, which may have been down to the Colonel's influence. The wedding was held at 9.41 am in a Las Vegas hotel, The Aladdin – as a temple of Mammon, it was about as far from nirvana as it is possible to get. There were few guests and no celebrities among them: just family and a selection of invited intimates that, interestingly, did not include some of his oldest, closest friends, notably Red West. In the wedding photographs, the King looks happy but his face is puffy and his eyes are baggy. The beginnings of a double chin are just discernible above his bow-tie. Priscilla looks doll-like, in heavy black eye make-up, and white lace. Never great travellers, the King and Queen honeymooned in Palm Springs, only to have their connubial bliss interrupted on the following day when

Elvis was called away to retake some dialogue on *Clambake*, his latest – and far from greatest – movie. But in the brief interlude that had been their wedding night, Priscilla had conceived. The King would have an heir.

Elvis's faith in astrology must have been confirmed when his first and only child was born nine months to the day after the wedding, on 1 February 1968. A little Aquarian at the dawning of the Age of Aquarius. Born at the Baptist Memorial hospital at 5.01 am, Lisa Marie weighed 6lb 14oz and inherited her parents' handsome looks. Elvis was instantly smitten. His own childhood stood him in good stead when it came to his turn to be a parent. He adored his daughter and always would. The new family was deliriously happy. They all went to Las Vegas where they watched Tom Jones perform, and then headed for the Hawaiian sun.

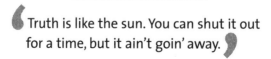

' Truth is like the sun. You can shut it out
for a time, but it ain't goin' away. '

But something was still missing in Elvis's life: live performance. He hadn't sung live to an audience for nearly a decade. Performing on stage had made him the artist he was, the rock and roll icon and breaker of cultural taboos. By following the green dollar signs to Hollywood, and blinkered by the Colonel, he had lost his electric connection to the audience and, with it, the chance to express himself fully through music.

Ironically, it was the Colonel who brought the King back to live performance. He sold the television company NBC the $1 million idea of Elvis's first TV special in eight years. What the Colonel had in mind was a Christmas extravaganza, full of carols and middle-of-the-road fare appropriate to the season. However, things turned out very differently. NBC wanted more than just a fireside festive show; rather than showcasing the cheesy, easy-listening performer the King had become, the station and its young director, Steve Binder, wanted to resurrect the real Elvis – the elemental performer who had shaken up a generation. The Colonel agreed to the format, providing that he got a Christmas single out of it. The NBC team had brought in the former Blue Moon Boys, Scotty Moore and DJ Fontana, who had been jettisoned in 1956 in favour of the Jordanaires, and choreographers and set designers who pulled out all the stops. Taped in two sixty-minute sessions, the result was a triumph. Elvis had always suffered from stage fright and the prospect of his first outing for nearly a decade in front of an audience must have terrified him. But he was slimmer than he had been for years and at his most beautiful. In his black leathers designed by Bill Belew – who from then on designed all Elvis's stage gear – he looked dangerously sexy and every inch the rock and roll icon everyone remembered.

Even if he didn't seem quite as confident as he had in pre-army days, his comeback performance was sensational and as near to the old Elvis as it was possible to get. The final number would be his Christmas single,

'If I Can Dream'. Written specially for the show, it spent thirteen weeks in the charts and heralded even better things to come. It was his biggest hit since 'Crying In The Chapel'. Broadcast by NBC in early December 1968, *Elvis* got mixed reviews but the viewers loved it. The show was a ratings-beating success that at last showed the King his way forward: he knew now that he just had to get back on the road.

Invigorated, Elvis was keen to get back to the studio and make music that had nothing to do with pulp movies, like *Charro!* and *The Trouble With Girls*, that he was still having to make in Hollywood. He landed up at American Studios thanks to three of his oldest friends: Marty Lacker, George Klein and Red West, all of whom had connections with the operation. The marathon sessions that resulted in the *Elvis In Memphis* album were the first he had recorded in the city since his Sun days. Comfortable back in his own milieu, he had the chance to work with producer Chips Moman, who co-ran the studio and acted as midwife to his real rebirth as a performer. The association gave him two of his best songs and biggest hits: 'In The Ghetto' and 'Suspicious Minds'.

The timing was perfect: his first Las Vegas performance thirteen years earlier had flopped. Now the town welcomed him and his material – old and new – with open arms. The month-long engagement arranged by the Colonel at the new, 2,000-seater International Hotel was a sell-out – more than 100,000 people paid $1,530,000 to see the King in concert.

> We do two show night for five weeks. A lotta times we'll go upstairs and sing until daylight – gospel songs. We grew up with it...it more or less puts your mind at ease. It does mine.
>
> FROM THE 1972 MGM DOCUMENTARY, *ELVIS ON TOUR*

This was just the start. After long years in the musical wilderness, Elvis was back on track. His mojo was working again.

DECLINE AND FALL

The 1970s is often called the decade that taste forgot and when it came to his stage costumes, Elvis certainly had his finger on the pulse. Bill Belew, whose inspired biker's leathers had worked so well on the TV special, created the first of the themed white jumpsuits that became the King's late-period trademark. To be fair to Belew, the idea was originally Elvis's. The shiny all-in-ones embellished gaudily with American motifs were light, easy to move around in, visible from the back of a stadium and very, very Las Vegas. Another advantage was that they streamlined the King's bulges.

Buoyed by a Number One smash with 'Suspicious Minds', his forty-eighth gold disc, Elvis geared up for the road. As the decade began, the calendar was full: a month in Las Vegas giving two shows a night, followed by six shows at the vast Houston Astrodome, where more than 200,000 fans saw him in a single week. Las Vegas was a triumph, the opening night studded with A-list stars who had flocked to see him.

Elvis resumed karate to keep fit and to give him something to focus on, under the instruction of martial arts master Ed Parker. Priscilla also began to study the discipline seriously. Since the birth of Lisa Marie, the Presleys' sex life had been non-existent. One of Elvis's phobias was that he could not or would not have sex with a woman who had given birth. Was it because any mother became too closely identified in his mind with his beloved Gladys? The King reverted to the kind of sexual encounters he was best at – flings with the groupies who lined up to entertain him after his shows, and a string of 'good girls' whom he taught to speak the baby language that was his mother tongue.

A frustrated Priscilla sought solace first with her dancing instructor and later with Hawaiian karate champion Mike Stone. Then Elvis got a fright. A waitress called Patricia Parker filed a paternity suit in Los Angeles, citing the star as the father of a child conceived after one of the Las Vegas shows. He denied having slept with her and filed a counter-claim, alleging that Parker was simply after his money. The court case took two years and a blood test, but Elvis won.

More drama followed two weeks later when a series of calls were made to The International Hotel, threatening at first to kill Elvis and then to kidnap him. Security staff were put on red alert and the FBI milled through the audience during his concerts, but nothing actually happened.

By now Elvis had a small collection of girlfriends – always virginal, sometimes interested in the same kind of spiritual quest as he was. Singer Kathy Westmoreland and actress Barbara Leigh, for example, both joined him on tour, though not at the same time. The King's first tour in twelve years took in St Louis, Detroit, Miami, Tampa and Mobile. His second, just two months later in November, covered California, Oklahoma and Washington State. It was a punishing schedule but at least he had something to look forward to in the form of his nightly love affair with the fans, who were as ardent as they had been in his 1950s heyday. Although he was only thirty-five, the tours were physically extremely demanding: the drugs kept him going.

In mid-1970 Elvis bought a gun collection and acquired a logo: the letters TCB arranged round a bolt of lightning. It was a visual pun – 'Takin' care of business – in a flash'. He had it made up into twelve solid gold pendants, one for himself and one for each of the Memphis Mafia. It was just the very thing for the 1970s medallion man – Elvis loved it and the logo would end up on his headstone.

His obsession with law enforcement (he was a special deputy several times over and had a collection of badges to prove it) took an even odder turn. The counter-culture and anti-Vietnam movement were in full swing; drugs were the enemy within. Elvis decided he must voice his concerns for the young of America to the man at the top. Wearing dark glasses and a full-length black leather coat, he embarked on a mission more reminiscent of Austin Powers than James Bond. At Memphis airport he bought a ticket to Washington DC in the false name of Jon Burrows. On arrival, he checked into a hotel then returned immediately to Memphis. Next day, he returned to Washington with two of the guys, Jerry Schilling and Sonny West, plus a California senator of his acquaintance, George Murphy. This time he travelled as John Carpenter, a character from his final film, *Change of Habit* (1969). On the flight, on American Airlines stationery, he wrote a letter in his child-like, looping script:

> '*Dear Mr President,*
> *First I would like to introduce myself. I am Elvis*
> *Presley ... I wish not to be given a title or an appointed*
> *position. I can and will do more good if I were made a*
> *Federal Agent at Large, and I will help best by doing it*
> *my way through my communications with people of all*
> *ages. First and Foremost I am an entertainer but all I*
> *need is the Federal Credentials.'*
>
> *Elvis Presley.*

LETTER, DECEMBER 19, 1970, TO PRESIDENT NIXON

He included his own and the Colonel's phone numbers and, marking it private and confidential, delivered the envelope to the White House at dawn.

It was an extraordinary thing to do. Was it genuine concern or had his mind been affected by his own drug consumption? We don't have a psychologist's insight but it was the first time Elvis's off-kilter behaviour had extended so far outside his own small world. However, Richard Nixon agreed to see him – the King had an audience with the President. When Elvis left the Oval Office, he had the federal narcotics agent's badge he had requested and had been sworn in by the president himself. The badge was the pride of his collection.

A more conventional honour came his way the day after his thirty-sixth birthday; he had told the president in his letter, as if to offer his credentials, that he was one of that year's nominees for the prestigious Jaycee Top Ten Young Men of the Year Award, not only for his services to entertainment but also to acknowledge his generous work for charity. He gave an estimated $20 million to good causes over his lifetime, much of it never publicized. Elvis received his gong on 16 January 1971 at Ellis Auditorium in Memphis from the then United Nations ambassador designate, George Bush. It was the first awards ceremony he had ever turned up for.

' When I was a child, ladies and gentlemen, I was a dreamer. I read comic books and I was the hero of the comic book. I saw movies and I was the hero in the movie. So every dream I ever dreamed has come true a hundred times. '
ELVIS, FROM HIS TOP TEN YOUNG MEN OF THE YEAR AWARDS ACCEPTANCE SPEECH

By the end of 1971, Priscilla had had enough and was ready to leave. She moved to Los Angeles with Mike Stone, taking Lisa Marie. Given that he hadn't honoured most of his marriage vows, this shouldn't have mattered much to Elvis, but it did. He might now have been free to bring whomever he liked home to his bed at Graceland but his pride was more than a little hurt. His drug consumption escalated and he threw himself into touring: in June 1972, he became the first artist to sell out Madison Square Garden in New York four nights in a row. Despite his burgeoning weight, he hadn't lost his appeal to women. A fortnight after he and Priscilla were formally separated, Elvis met twenty-two-year-old beauty queen Linda Thompson in Memphis. She was his next serious girlfriend, trained in all his favourite ways – adept at baby talk, playing 'mommy' to his 'baby' and making sure he didn't choke on half-eaten food when he fell asleep stoned. She would also try to save the King from himself – and fail, for he had set his course towards his final destination.

The touring programme grew almost manic, the costumes more outrageous. For his *Aloha From Hawaii Via Satellite* special in 1973, which was watched by a record billion viewers round the world, the white jumpsuits were decorated with the eagle emblem and a cape attached to the shoulders – Elvis as Captain America. To prepare for the show, he had gone on an extreme crash diet and paid the price. On tour, he was taking enough to tranquillize an elephant – depressants, sleeping draughts, and anything else that caught his fancy from the

Physician's Desk Reference. But he was forgetting lyrics on stage, looking puffy and tired and even dissolving into giggles as he sang. The King was losing the plot.

Six days after his divorce from Priscilla in October 1973, Elvis collapsed after having trouble breathing on the plane home to Memphis from Los Angeles. Swollen and bloated, he had a range of problems attributable to serious long-term drug abuse. His system had begun to collapse under the strain. He was admitted to Baptist Memorial hospital in Memphis and weaned off his habit under strict supervision, Linda by his side. He still had his spiritual texts and studied them avidly at night. Soon he had recovered enough to go home, and appeared to be healthy.

His personal physician, Dr George Nichopoulos or Dr Nick, monitored him closely but Elvis was still an addict and wasn't undertaking any kind of 12-step programme. Like all addicts, he didn't want to admit he had a problem. His health went downhill fast; he had wild mood swings and alternated between depression, generous bouts of gift-giving and rage. He would lock himself into the bathroom or his bedroom and stay there for hours. In performance, he launched into stream-of-consciousness nonsense between numbers. Rumours began to appear in the press about his drug use. Instead of taking care of himself, he kept touring relentlessly, filling stadiums and his own and the Colonel's pockets. This lifestyle can hardly have been fun, but it was a pattern he maintained until the end. He should have been in his prime but he was a mess: three days before his last tour, weighing nearly nineteen stones, Elvis was trying in despair to shed three stones so that he would pass for fit on stage.

Linda had gone, replaced by Ginger Alden, his last 'mommy' and, at nineteen, too young to know what she had got herself into. But Ginger gave the King his last few months of happiness and a new project to look forward to: marriage. Sadly, Elvis was too far down the path of self-destruction to turn back.

> I never realized anything like this was possible, that I'd ever be in Hawaii or Las Vegas or Hollywood. It's quite a change to jump into this stuff. If you're not careful, you'll crack up.
> 1950s

Had he remembered his own words, perhaps the world's first rock-and-roll superstar would have survived.

The end, when it came, was sudden and miserably undignified. In the early hours of 16 August 1977, he was suffering from the acute insomnia that had plagued him since his youth. Though he still had his own hair and teeth, the beautiful boy had turned into a fat forty-two-year-old. Morbidly obese, he was failing miserably to get down to performing weight despite fasting on fruit and water. But he was happy because Lisa Marie was visiting and there was much to look forward to: he was thinking about announcing his engagement to Ginger on the last night of the tour. His usual dosage did not relieve his state of wakefulness that night. Even a game of racketball in the small hours with his cousin Billy didn't tire him. During the night, he took three separate cocktails of prescription drugs designed to help him relax and sleep, but none of them worked. At 9 am, he went into the bathroom with a book on the Shroud of Turin and a warning from Ginger not to fall asleep with the door locked. She nodded off herself and woke in the early afternoon – but where was Elvis? A knock on the bathroom door produced no reply. When she looked inside, the King was on the shag-piled floor in front of the lavatory, gold pajamas round his ankles, face-down in a pool of vomit. He was rushed to hospital but it was too late. Elvis was pronounced dead at 3.30 pm, on 16 August 1977.

An autopsy found extensive internal damage to his arteries, heart and digestive system and evidence that he had taken fourteen different drugs in massive quantities. The official conclusion was that he had died of a heart attack although the drugs he had taken must have taken their toll. The federal narc had OD'd.

Elvis lies buried in a copper coffin in the meditation garden at Graceland, next to Gladys, Vernon and Jesse Garon. But the King is not dead. The myth is that he lives on in an anonymous little town somewhere, that he simply wanted to escape the intolerable pressures of what his life had become. The truth is that he does live on – in hearts and minds everywhere.

A BIG HUNK O' LOVE:
Elvis's

Elvis never had problems attracting women, even as an adolescent with bad skin. He never had to suffer the torment of unrequited crushes that is the lot of the average teenager. And once he had blossomed into his god-like prime, he never looked back. But he did have serious hang-ups that affected his sexual behaviour and, consequently, his relationships.

There were hundreds, if not thousands, of women over the years but only a few who really mattered to Elvis. Although Gladys loved her son obsessively, she never tried to stop him from enjoying romantic relationships. She was extremely fond of several girlfriends, especially Dixie Locke, June Juanico and Anita Wood. But it was Gladys who gave Elvis his confidence and she was the most important woman in his life until Priscilla Beaulieu, the only woman he married. The King was never monogamous which must have been hard for his long-term partners to endure; he could also be jealous and threw tantrums when he didn't get his own way, especially in the last five years of his life. Materially, he was extremely generous and gave expensive trinkets, clothing and cars, especially when he was wooing. He was never a slow burner; his usual pattern of behaviour was to fall for someone instantly, lavish attention and gifts on her, then when she began to return his feelings, Elvis's ardour would cool and he would go off and see other women, while keeping the long-term lover in place. He rarely took responsibility for ending relationships and usually left it to the women, although he sometimes allowed things to peter out. Of his four most important relationships, the only one Elvis ended was with Linda.

Perhaps because of his relationship with Gladys, there was a part of Elvis that was destined not to grow up – the boy inside him who never quite matured. For the women who really loved him, that was part of the attraction. Yes, he was one of the world's richest and most famous men. Yes, he was tall, dark and, until his last few years, extremely handsome. But he possessed an extra element that was a potent aphrodisiac: his little-boy-lost vulnerability. Whatever he got up to with the groupies and showgirls that passed in the night, Elvis the romantic was a younger self, who related to the female of the species on a child-like, playful – albeit sexual – level. Although there were relationships with his peers, notably the actress Ann-Margret, whom he met on the set of *Viva Las Vegas* in 1963 and with whom he enjoyed an intense affair, after his mother's death he generally preferred his girls as young as possible: they had to be pretty and petite, like little dolls. (He was unable to relate sexually in any way to women who had given birth: he found it a turn-off, as Priscilla found to her cost.)

He respected virginity as a state of grace and innocence and however far things went, it is well documented that 'horseplay' and kissing went on at the very least. This sort of behaviour would cause a scandal today and it might have been then had it become public, as Jerry Lee Lewis discovered when the British press found out that he had brought his underage bride on tour with him. But Elvis, like Jerry Lee, also hailed from hillbilly stock – a culture in which it was not unusual for an adult man to pair up with a nubile teenager. Ultimately, although he fell in love many times, he was a true mother's boy and as he himself said: Gladys was his best girl.

Anita Wood (1957 – 1962)

Anita was a petite nineteen-year-old blonde singer whose ambition was to act, but in 1957 she was working on a music television show in Memphis. There she met Elvis's friend, George Klein, who arranged an introduction by telephone. Anita already had a date for the evening when the King called and, instead of cancelling her previous appointment, she apologized to Elvis and said she couldn't make it. Luckily, Elvis was intrigued by her ethics and rang again a fortnight later. This time they clicked over cheeseburgers in the private dining room at his favourite restaurant. That night he discovered that Anita was a 'good girl' who most certainly would not 'go all the way'– music to Elvis's ears and confirmation that she was worthy of his attentions. To add to his pleasure, Gladys gave Anita the seal of approval and became extremely fond of her.

Although he presented Anita with a huge diamond and sapphire ring, it was not an engagement token. The couple had been photographed together frequently, though, and the Colonel stepped in to nip marriage rumours in the bud. It would not do for his boy's image at this stage in his career to be anything but young, free and single – it would upset the fans and therefore business. Elvis was told to keep the relationship with Anita quiet. In September 1957, she entered and won a talent show: the Hollywood Star Hunt. It was her big opportunity but the only A-list she would ever be on was Elvis's. She was cast in a film but the production company went bust, and she gave up her dream, to return to Memphis and Elvis, although she continued to work in television – when Gladys died, she was working on the *Andy Williams Show* in New York.

While Elvis was in Germany, the two kept in touch. Anita knew that there were other girls, especially in Hollywood, but also that she was special to him. Back in civilian life, he gave her a beautiful diamond necklace. But the Elvis who came out of the army wasn't the same man she had waved off to Europe. Priscilla's arrival in America was the last straw. Anita began to realize that, even after five years, Elvis wasn't going to change and that he probably wasn't going to marry her. She ended the relationship in the kitchen at Graceland and Elvis didn't put up any resistance.

> Guys, I've just met the prettiest girl I've ever seen. Her name is Priscilla. Some day I'll probably marry her.

Priscilla Beaulieu Presley (1959 – 1972)

Elvis would be no more faithful to his wife than he was to anyone else. He first laid eyes on fourteen-year-old Priscilla Beaulieu when she walked through the door of his sitting room at Bad Nauheim in Germany, in her neat sailor dress. In the looks department, Priscilla was blessed with strong, exquisite bone structure and, even in her mid-teens, possessed a natural poise that accentuated her already obvious beauty. She looked like a teenage dream. She was also intelligent. Currie Grant, who had brought her along, may not have known that he was making history, but he must have known that Elvis would be more than happy to meet Priscilla.

Although ten years older, the still-grieving Elvis was captivated the moment he saw her. And if Priscilla didn't quite understand the implications of his feelings, she knew that she was thrilled to meet her idol and was soon in the full throes of a crush. Unlike most teen crushes, this one was reciprocated. With the permission of her parents, and on the strict understanding that she would be chaperoned, she was soon spending most evenings with Elvis, and enjoying a level of intimacy that would have horrified her parents had they known. That Christmas, he gave her a gold watch studded with diamonds. When he finished his army service and returned to the US, Priscilla went to see him off – it was the last she would see of Elvis for nearly three years. But he was thinking about her as much as she was dreaming of him. It was arranged with her parents, after a rollercoaster charm-offensive and sincere assurances that she would be properly looked after, that Priscilla would visit him for a two-week holiday in Los Angeles: she would be staying with family friends, for propriety's sake. In practice, she stayed with him and had a ball. Elvis showed her all his favourite haunts and took her shopping for glamorous outfits and make-up and had her thick, glossy hair restyled. He had begun the process of moulding the sixteen-year-old into his perfect woman: a mirror image of himself.

After a further visit to Graceland at Christmas, where she cemented her growing closeness to Elvis's grandmother, Minnie Mae, an audacious plan was hatched that thrilled the two lovers: her family was being posted back to the US – since they wanted to be together, why shouldn't Priscilla finish school in Memphis? So, after much negotiation with the Beaulieus, Priscilla moved in with Vernon and his new wife, Dee Stanley, on the periphery of Graceland, attending school until she graduated. Soon she moved into the main house, where she and Elvis created their own cosy little world where they both felt happy and safe – in spirit not unlike the one he had shared with his parents when he was growing up. They may have been happy but they didn't marry until 1967, when the King was thirty-two and his princess twenty-two. A simple secular ceremony, held on 1 May at The Aladdin Hotel in Las Vegas, was attended by Vernon and Dee and a small number of friends, followed by a wedding breakfast fit for the King and his Queen; they honeymooned in Palm Springs. On the day, the pair looked as if they had been made for each other: two dark-haired beauties with perfect teeth. An evening of bliss lay ahead for them – according to Priscilla's memoirs, although the relationship had been sexual since not long after their first meeting, it was not consummated until their wedding night. And as if by magic, their first and only child, Lisa Marie, was born nine months later to the day, on 1 February 1968.

The royal household was now complete and for a while happiness reigned at Graceland and in Los Angeles where they also had a home. But the marriage was only to last five years. Not only were they rarely alone, thanks to the ever-present extended family and assorted Memphis Mafiosi but Elvis was frequently away. And eventually there were the rumours of other women: Elvis liked to have his cake and eat it too. Priscilla tried hard – she even took up karate, which was Elvis's favourite recreational hobby, and studied it seriously. But what really drove them apart was that Priscilla grew up. Elvis may have thought he could groom a young girl into a perfect wife but he couldn't bend her personality to his will. She was thinking for herself, and didn't like some of her conclusions. In February 1972, Priscilla abdicated from the Queen's throne. After thirteen years with Elvis, five of them as Mrs Presley, she had had enough. She told him their marriage was over, and left him for karate champion Mike Stone. She took Lisa Marie and when Elvis filed for divorce, didn't contest. Priscilla would have custody of their only child, but Elvis had open visiting rights and was an active, involved, adoring father to the last. Priscilla, who became an actress, most notably in the 1980s soap *Dallas* and the film *Naked Gun*, kept her married name and continued her association with the King at one remove; she was one of the executors of his estate and is now the official guardian of the Presley image and estate.

Linda Thompson (1972 – 1976)

Linda, a Memphis girl, was a bubbly, bright university drop-out and beauty queen – the reigning Miss Tennessee – when she met Elvis one summer night, five months after his split with Priscilla. After two dates, the twenty-two-year-old Linda went on holiday for three weeks with her parents. Her absence only whetted the King's appetite, especially as he had been unable to contact her. By the time she got back, he was waiting at the airport – unusual for Elvis, who usually sent a minion to pick up his women rather than go himself. He was completely smitten.

Linda put her career plans on hold – she had intended to head for New York to act or get into modelling – to devote herself to the King. Although this was the period in which he would begin his drug-fuelled decline, this was a relationship that gave him a great deal of happiness, in the first lovestruck months at least. Linda was not only stunning to look at, an entertaining companion and deeply attractive to Elvis, she got on well with everyone at Graceland. Despite her youth, she had the mental resources to counter the King's darker moods. Elvis, who was increasingly in the habit of reverting to poor-little-boy mode, also awakened her maternal instinct. Linda became the perfect Gladys-substitute: he called her 'Mommy' and the couple adopted the same kind of baby language Elvis had learned at his real mother's knee.

Eventually, as tended to happen with the King's women, Linda also grew up. Living comfortably was not enough of a return for the amount of energy it took to keep Elvis, who was by now seriously addicted to drugs, happy and in the land of the living. In the end, he pulled the plug but, by the time he did, Linda was more than ready to move on.

Ginger Alden (December 1976 – August 1977)

Ginger was Elvis's last lover. At only twenty, she was ill-equipped to deal with the King in the sick, bloated, debauched months of his final decline. Flame-haired, she was one of a trio of Alden girls, all extremely pretty; beauty queen Ginger had been crowned Miss Traffic Safety and Miss Mid-South and her older sister Terry was Miss Tennessee. Although all three were paraded before the King, Elvis homed in on Ginger. He certainly knew how to impress a naïve southern belle. On their first date, he took her for a drive in his $35,000 Stutz Blackhawk sports car to the airport, where he suggested a ride in his private jet. On board, he told her they were flying all the way to Las Vegas. Ginger was worried – she would have to tell her mother. Elvis reassured her that she could call when they got there. Instead of being angry, Mrs Alden was delighted and encouraged her daughter to accept the King's attentions. Thereafter Elvis lavished gifts on Ginger and wooed her avidly. Lonely, and perhaps sensing that his charms were fast diminishing, he quickly decided to marry her. Only two months after their first meeting, he consulted his numerology bible to ensure that he chose the right moment on the most auspicious day: on 27 January, he took Ginger to the bathroom and sat her in the reading chair beside the lavatory. Down on one knee on the shag pile, he proposed, presenting a huge diamond ring made from an 11.5 carat gem he had worn himself. By now convinced she was in love, Ginger accepted. They were engaged.

Elvis would not have expected Ginger – a 'good girl' – to give up her virginity, but any kind of strenuous sexual activity was, in any case, unlikely to have been on the cards. At only forty-two, Elvis was well past his prime thanks to the increasingly potent drug cocktails he took every night: the quantities of medication he was on would not have enhanced his libido. In the end it was Ginger who found his body, grotesquely frozen in *rigor mortis* into a foetal position on the bathroom floor, next to the chair in which she had sat seven months before, as the King proposed to her.

The World According to Elvis

ON FOOD:
'When I have meat for dinner I like it well done.
I ain't ordering a pet.'

ON RELIGION:
'I think it's more important to believe in God than goin' to
church.'

'I don't want to miss out on heaven because of a technicality.'
(ASKED WHY HE WORE A CHRISTIAN CROSS,
A STAR OF DAVID AND A HEBREW CHI)

ON FAME AND SUCCESS:
'I know that the Lord can give and the Lord can take away.
I might be herding sheep next year.'

'I have no use for bodyguards, but I have a very special use
for two highly trained certified public accountants.'

'Adversity is sometimes hard upon a man; but for one man
who can stand prosperity, there are a hundred that will
stand adversity.'

'Ambition is a dream with a V8 engine.'

'The thing I like about success is to know that you've got so many friends, a lot of real close friends that I've made since I've been in the business.'

ON ONE OF HIS HEROES:
'I knew by heart all the dialogue of James Dean's films; I could watch *Rebel Without a Cause* a hundred times over.'

ON HIS CRITICS:
'Gossip is small words from small minds.'

'People who read sex into my music have dirty minds. I've always lived a straight, clean life. I don't set any kind of bad example.'

'I got sick one night, I had a temperature of 102 and they wouldn't let me perform. From three different sources I heard I was strung out on heroin. I had the flu. If I find the individual who has said that about me, I'm gonna break your goddam neck...It is dangerous, damaging to myself, to my little daughter, to my father, to my friends and to my fans.'

ON THE MEMPHIS MAFIA:
'This is my corporation which travels with me all the time. More than that, all these members of my corporation are my friends.'

ON SINGING:
'My voice alone is just an ordinary voice. What people come to see is how I use it. If I stand still while I'm singing, I'm dead!'

ON MUSIC AND PERFORMING:
'Rock 'n' roll is a music. Why should a music contribute to juvenile delinquency?" If people are gonna be delinquents, they're gonna be delinquents if they hear *Mother Goose* rhymes. Rock 'n' roll does not contribute to juvenile delinquency at all.'

'Anything that don't frighten the children is in good taste, far as I'm concerned.'

'I watch my audience and listen to them and I know that we're all gettin' somethin' out of our system. None of us knows what it is – the important thing is we're getting rid of it and nobody's gettin' hurt.'

'People ask me where I got my singing style. I didn't copy my style from anybody...Country music was always an influence on my kind of music.'
(FROM *THE BOOK OF COUNTRY MUSIC WISDOM*, ED. BY CRISWELL FREEMAN, 1994)

'When rock 'n' roll dies out another type of emotional music is going to take its place. Then I can sit on my back porch at Graceland and remember the good ol' days.'

'A live concert to me is exciting because of all the electricity that is generated in the crowd and on stage. It's my favourite part of the business – live concerts.'
(AT A PRESS CONFERENCE BEFORE HIS 1973 TELEVISION SPECIAL, *ELVIS: ALOHA FROM HAWAII, VIA SATELLITE*)

'You have to put on a show for people in order to draw a crowd. If I just stood out there and sang and didn't move a muscle, then people would say, "My goodness, I can stay home and listen to his records." You have to give them a show.'

'I've never gotten over what they call stage fright. I go through it every show. I'm pretty concerned, I'm pretty much thinking about the show. I never get completely comfortable with it, and I don't let the people around me get comfortable with it, in that I remind them it's a new crowd out there, it's a new audience, and they haven't seen us before. So it's got to be like the first time we go on.'
FROM A 1972 TAPED INTERVIEW USED IN MGM'S DOCUMENTARY, *ELVIS ON TOUR*

ON RACISM:
'If you hate another human being because of their race, you're hating part of yourself.'

Elvis According to the World

'Nothing really affected me until Elvis.' – JOHN LENNON

'He taught white America how to get down.' – JAMES BROWN

'Elvis is the best ever, the most original. He started the ball rolling for us all.' – JIM MORRISON

'I remember Elvis as a young man hanging round the Sun studios. Even then I knew this kid had a tremendous talent. He was a dynamic young boy. His phraseology, his way of looking at a song, was as unique as Sinatra's. I was a tremendous fan and had Elvis lived, there would have been no end to his inventiveness.' – BB KING

'There have been a lotta tough guys. There have been pretenders and there have been contenders. But there is only one King.' – BRUCE SPRINGSTEEN

'The highlight of my career? That's easy. Elvis recording one of my songs.' – BOB DYLAN

'A lot of people have accused Elvis of stealing the black man's music when, in fact, almost every black solo entertainer copied his stage mannerisms from Elvis.'
– JACKIE WILSON

'I'm just a singer but Elvis was the embodiment of the whole American culture. Life just wouldn't have been the same without him.' – FRANK SINATRA

'You have no idea how great he is, really you don't. You have no comprehension – it's absolutely impossible. I can't tell you why he's so great, but he is. He's sensational.'
– PHIL SPECTOR

'Elvis is the greatest blues singer in the world today.'
– JOE COCKER

'If Elvis copied me, I don't care. More power to him. I'm not starving.' – BO DIDDLEY

'There was something just bordering on rudeness about Elvis. He never actually did anything rude, but he always seemed as if he was just going to. On a scale of one to ten, I would rate him eleven.' – SAMMY DAVIS JUNIOR

'He was an integrator. Elvis was a blessing. They wouldn't let black music through. He opened the door for black music.' – LITTLE RICHARD

'No one, but no one, is his equal or ever will be. He was and is supreme.' – MICK JAGGER

'People like myself, Mick Jagger and the others only really followed in his footsteps.' – ROD STEWART

ELVIS ACCORDING TO THE WORLD

'Elvis is my man.' – JANIS JOPLIN

'He was an instinctive actor. He was quite bright... He was very intelligent. He was not a punk. He was very elegant, sedate and refined, and sophisticated.' – WALTER MATTHAU

'I thought anyone who had been the centre of all that insanity for so long would have some of it rub off on him. But, after working on *Change Of Habit* with him, I realized I'd never worked with a more gentlemanly, kinder man. He's gorgeous.' – MARY TYLER MOORE

'The first time I heard his music back in '54 or '55, I was in a car and I heard the announcer say: "Here's a guy who, when he appears on stage in the South, the girls scream and rush the stage." Then he played 'That's All Right (Mama)'. I thought his name was about the weirdest I'd ever heard. I thought for sure he was a black guy. Later on I grew my hair like him, imitated his stage act. Once I went all over New York looking for a lavender shirt like the one he wore on one of his albums. I felt wonderful when he sang 'Bridge Over Troubled Water', even though it was a touch on the dramatic side – but so was the song.'
– PAUL SIMON

'It was a real thrill sitting there with the King. He was always one of my favourites. I always knew that no matter how I felt, if I played an Elvis record it would make me happy. I've always dreamed of producing an album for Elvis.'
– PAUL MCCARTNEY

'Even back then, when people would laugh at his sideburns and his pink coat and call him cissy, he had a pretty hard road to go. In some areas, motorcycle gangs would come to the shows. They would come to get Elvis, but he never worried about it. He went right out and did his thing and before the show was over, they were standing in line to get his autograph too.' – CARL PERKINS

'When he started, he couldn't spell Tennessee. Now he owns it.' – BOB HOPE

'He never contributed a damn thing to music' – BING CROSBY

'Elvis was the first and the best. He is my favourite of all time.' – BILL CLINTON

'I love his music because he was my generation. But then again, Elvis is everyone's generation and he always will be.' – MARGARET THATCHER

'He epitomized America and for that we shall be eternally grateful. There will never be anyone else like him. Let's all rejoice in his music.' – RONALD REAGAN

'He was ahead of his time because he had such deep feelings. He had the privilege of deep feelings because he was deeply loved by this mother, Gladys. He was able to appreciate profound beauty in sounds. And he started a musical revolution. They say all revolutions start from love.' – IMELDA MARCOS

'I think Elvis is the sexiest man to ever walk the earth. I love him.' – BRITNEY SPEARS

'He inspired me to be a performer. He is a legend, the King.' – ROBBIE WILLIAMS

'If life was fair, Elvis would be alive and all the impersonators would be dead.' – JOHNNY CARSON

'The first time I met him I was blown away. I just looked at him and said: "Damn, son, you about the best-looking thing I ever did see, kinda wish I was a girl right now, Elvis."' – JERRY REED, COUNTRY SINGER

Discography/Filmography

ELVIS SINGLES
All singles were issued at both 45 & 78 rpm until 1958

1954   That's All Right (Mama) /
        Blue Moon Of Kentucky *(issued on 6 July)*

1954   Good Rockin' Tonight /
        I Don't Care If The Sun Don't Shine

1955   Milkcow Blues Boogie / You're a Heartbreaker

1955   Baby, Let's Play House /
        I'm Left, You're Right, She's Gone

1955   Mystery Train / I Forgot To Remember To Forget

1956   Heartbreak Hotel / I Was The One

1956   Hound Dog / Don't Be Cruel

1956   Love Me Tender / Any Way You Want Me

1956   Blue Suede Shoes / Tutti Frutti

1956   I Got A Woman / I'm Counting On You

1956   I'll Never Let You Go /
          I'm Gonna Sit Right Down And Cry (Over You)

1956   Tryin' To Get To You / I Love You Because

1956   Blue Moon / Just Because

1956   Money Honey / One-Sided Love Affair

1956   Lawdy, Miss Clawdy / Shake, Rattle And Roll

1957   Too Much / Playing For Keeps

1957   All Shook Up / That's When Your Heartaches Begin

1957   (Let Me Be Your) Teddy Bear / Loving You

1957   Jailhouse Rock / Treat Me Nice

1958   Don't / I Beg Of You

1958   Wear My Ring Around Your Neck /
          Don'cha Think It's Time?

1958   Hard-Headed Woman / Don't Ask Me Why

1958   One Night /I Got Stung *(last to be issued as a 78)*

1959   A Fool Such As I / I Need Your Love Tonight

1959   A Big Hunk O' Love / My Wish Came True

1960   Stuck On You / Fame And Fortune

1960   It's Now Or Never / A Mess Of Blues

1960   Are You Lonesome Tonight? / I Gotta Know

1961   Surrender / Lonely Man

1961   I Feel So Bad / Wild In The Country

1961   (Marie's The Name) His Latest Flame / Little Sister

1961   Can't Help Falling In Love / Rock-A-Hula Baby

1962   Good Luck Charm / Anything That's Part Of You

1962   She's Not You / Just Tell Her Jim Said Hello

1962   Return To Sender / Where Do You Come From?

1963   One Broken Heart For Sale /
They Remind Me Too Much Of You

1963   Bossa Nova Baby / Witchcraft

1963   Kissin' Cousins / It Hurts Me

1964   Kiss Me Quick / Suspicion

1964   What'd I Say? / Viva Las Vegas

1964   Such A Night / Never Ending

1964   Ain't That Loving You, Baby? / Ask Me

1965   Do The Clam / You'll Be Gone

1965   Crying In The Chapel /
        I Believe In The Man In The Sky

1965   (Such An) Easy Question / It Feels So Right

1965   I'm Yours / Long Lonely Highway

1965   Puppet On A String / Wooden Heart

1965   Blue Christmas / Santa Claus Is Back In Town

1966   Tell Me Why / Blue River

1966   Joshua Fit The Battle / Known Only To Him

1966   Milky White Way / Swing Down Sweet Chariot

1966   Frankie And Johnny / Please Don't Stop Loving Me

1966   Love Letters / Come What May

1966   Spinout / All That I Am

1966   If Every Day Was Like Christmas /
        How Would You Like To Be?

1967   Indescribably Blue / Fools Fall In Love

1967   There's Always Me / Judy

1967   Big Boss Man / You Don't Know Me

1968   Guitar Man / High Heel Sneakers

1968   US Male / Stay Away

1968   You'll Never Walk Alone / We Call On Him

1968   Your Time Hasn't Come Yet Baby /
        Let Yourself Go

1968   Almost In Love / A Little Less Conversation

1968   If I Can Dream / Edge Of Reality

1969   Memories / Charro

1969   His Hand In Mine / How Great Thou Art

1969   Clean Up Your Own Back Yard /
        The Fair Is Moving On[*]

1969   Suspicious Minds / You'll Think Of Me

1969   Don't Cry Daddy / Rubberneckin'

1970   Kentucky Rain / My Little Friend

1970   The Wonder Of You / Mama Liked The Roses

1970   I've Lost You / The Next Step Is Love

1970   You Don't Have To Say You Love Me / Patch It Up

1970   I Really Don't Want To Know /
       There Goes My Everything

1971   Rags To Riches / Where Did They Go, Lord?

1971   Life / Only Believe

1971   I'm Leavin' / Heart Of Rome

1971   It's Only Love / The Sound Of Your Cry

1971   Merry Christmas, Baby / O Come, All Ye Faithful

1972   Until It's Time For You To Go /
       We Can Make The Morning

1972   He Touched Me / Bosom Of Abraham

1972   An American Trilogy /
       The First Time Ever I Saw Your Face

1972   Burning Love / It's A Matter Of Time

1972   Separate Ways / Always On My Mind

1973   Steamroller Blues / The Fool

1973   Raised On Rock / For Old Times' Sake

1974   I've Got A Think About You, Baby /
        Take Good Care Of Her

1974   If You Talk In Your Sleep / Help Me

1974   Promised Land / It's Midnight

1975   My Boy / Thinking About You

1975   T-R-O-U-B-L-E / Mr. Songman

1976   Hurt / For The Heart

1976   Moody Blue / She Thinks I Still Care

1977   Way Down / Pledging My Love

Elvis EPs

1956   *ELVIS PRESLEY (DOUBLE EP):*
        SIDE 1: Blue Suede Shoes; I'm Counting On You;
        SIDE 2: I Got A Woman; One-Sided Love Affair
        SIDE 3: Tutti Frutti; Tryin' To Get To You;
        SIDE 4: I'm Gonna Sit Right Down And Cry (Over
        You); I'll Never Let You Go

1956   *ELVIS PRESLEY:*
        SIDE 1: Blue Suede Shoes; Tutti Frutti
        SIDE 2: I Got A Woman; Just Because

1956   *HEARTBREAK HOTEL:*
        SIDE 1: Heartbreak Hotel; I Was The One
        SIDE 2: Money Honey; I Forgot To Remember To Forget

1956   *THE REAL ELVIS:*
        SIDE 1: Don't Be Cruel; I Want You, I Need You, I Love You
        SIDE 2: Hound Dog; My Baby Left Me

1956   *ELVIS PRESLEY:*
        SIDE 1: Shake, Rattle And Roll; I Love You Because
        SIDE 2: Blue Moon; Lawdy, Miss Clawdy

1956   *ANY WAY YOU WANT ME:*
        SIDE 1: Any Way You Want Me; I'm Left, You're Right,
        She's Gone
        SIDE 2: I Don't Care If The Sun Don't Shine; Mystery
        Train

1956 *ELVIS VOL. 1:*
SIDE 1: Rip It Up; Love Me
SIDE 2: When My Blue Moon Turns To Gold Again;
Paralyzed

1956 *LOVE ME TENDER:*
SIDE 1: Love Me Tender; Let Me
SIDE 2: Poor Boy; We're Gonna Move

1956 *ELVIS VOL. 2:*
SIDE 1: So Glad You're Mine; Old Shep
SIDE 2: Ready Teddy; Anyplace Is Paradise

1957 *STRICTLY ELVIS:*
SIDE 1: Long Tall Sally; First In Line
SIDE 2: How Do You Think I Feel?; How's The World
Treating You

1957 *PEACE IN THE VALLEY:*
SIDE 1: (There'll Be) Peace In The Valley (For Me);
It Is No Secret
SIDE 2: I Believe; Take My Hand, Precious Lord

1957 *JUST FOR YOU:*
SIDE 1: I Need You So; Have I Told You Lately That I
Love You?
SIDE 2: Blueberry Hill; Is It So Strange?

1957   *LOVING YOU, VOL. 1:*
      SIDE 1: Loving You; Party
      SIDE 2: (Let Me Be Your) Teddy Bear; True Love

1957   *LOVING YOU, VOL. 2:*
      SIDE 1: Lonesome Cowboy; Hot Dog
      SIDE 2: Mean Woman Blues; Got A Lot O' Livin' To Do

1957   *JAILHOUSE ROCK:*
      SIDE 1: Jailhouse Rock; Young And Beautiful
      SIDE 2: I Want To Be Free; Don't Leave Me Now;
      Baby, I Don't Care

1957   *ELVIS SINGS CHRISTMAS SONGS:*
      SIDE 1: Santa, Bring My Baby Back (To Me); Blue
      Christmas
      SIDE 2: Santa Claus Is Back In Town; I'll Be Home For
      Christmas

1958   *KING CREOLE VOL. 1:*
      SIDE 1: King Creole; New Orleans
      SIDE 2: As Long As I Have You; Lover Doll

1958   *KING CREOLE VOL. 2:*
      SIDE 1: Trouble; Young Dreams
      SIDE 2: Crawfish; Dixieland Rock

1958   *CHRISTMAS WITH ELVIS:*
      SIDE 1: White Christmas; Here Comes Santa Claus
      SIDE 2: O Little Town Of Bethlehem; Silent Night

1959   *A TOUCH OF GOLD. VOL. 1:*
        SIDE 1: Hard-Headed Woman; Good Rocking Tonight
        SIDE 2: Don't; I Beg Of You

1959   *A TOUCH OF GOLD VOL. 2:*
        SIDE 1: Wear My Ring Around Your Neck;
        Treat Me Nice
        SIDE 2: One Night; That's All Right (Mama)

1960   *A TOUCH OF GOLD, VOL. 3:*
        SIDE 1: Too Much; All Shook Up
        SIDE 2: Don't Ask Me Why; Blue Moon Of Kentucky

1961   *ELVIS BY REQUEST – FLAMING STAR:*
        SIDE 1: Flaming Star; Summer Kisses, Winter Tears
        SIDE 2: Are You Lonesome Tonight?; It's Now Or
        Never

1962   *FOLLOW THAT DREAM:*
        SIDE 1: Follow That Dream; Angel
        SIDE 2: What A Wonderful Life; I'm Not The Marrying
        Kind

1962   *KID GALAHAD:*
        SIDE 1: King Of The Whole Wide World; This Is Living;
        Riding The Rainbow
        SIDE 2: Home Is Where The Heart Is; I Got Lucky; A
        Whistling Tune

1964   *VIVA LAS VEGAS:*
SIDE 1: If You Think I Don't Need You; I Need
Somebody To Lean On
SIDE 2: C'mon Everybody; Today, Tomorrow And
Forever

1965   *TICKLE ME:*
SIDE 1: I Feel That I've Known You Forever; Slowly
But Surely
SIDE 2: Night Rider; Put The Blame On Me; Dirty,
Dirty Feeling

1967   *EASY COME, EASY GO:*
SIDE 1: Easy Come, Easy Go; The Love Machine; Yoga
Is As Yoga Does
SIDE 2: You Gotta Stop; Sing You Children; I'll Take
Love

ELVIS LPs

1956   *ELVIS PRESLEY:*
SIDE 1: Blue Suede Shoes; I'm Counting On You; I Got A Woman; One-Sided Love Affair; I Love You Because; Just Because
SIDE 2: Tutti Frutti; Tryin' To Get To You; I'm Gonna Sit Right Down And Cry (Over you); I'll Never Let You Go; Blue Moon; Money Honey

1956   *ELVIS:*
SIDE 1: Rip It Up; Love Me; When My Blue Moon Turns To Gold Again; Long Tall Sally; First In Love; Paralyzed
SIDE 2: So Glad You're Mine; Old Shep; Ready Teddy; Anyplace Is Paradise; How's The World Treating Me?; How Do You Think I Feel?

1957   *LOVING YOU:*
SIDE 1: Mean Woman Blues; (Let Me Be Your) Teddy Bear; Loving You; Got A Lot O' Livin' To Do; Lonesome Cowboy; Hot Dog; Party
SIDE 2: Blueberry Hill; True Love; Don't Leave Me Now; Have I Told You Lately That I Love You?; I Need You So

1957   *ELVIS' CHRISTMAS ALBUM:*
SIDE 1: Santa Claus Is Back In Town; White Christmas; Here Comes Santa Claus; I'll Be Home For Christmas; Blue Christmas; Santa, Bring My Baby Back

135

SIDE 2: O Little Town Of Bethlehem; Silent Night; (There'll Be) Peace In The Valley; I Believe; Take My Hand, Precious Lord; It's No Secret

1958 *ELVIS GOLDEN RECORDS VOL. 1:*
SIDE 1: Hound Dog; Loving You; All Shook Up; Heartbreak Hotel; Jailhouse Rock; Love Me; Too Much
SIDE 2: Don't Be Cruel; That's When Your Heartaches Begin; (Let Me Be Your) Teddy Bear; Love Me Tender; Treat Me Nice; Anyway You Want Me; I Want You, I Need You, I Love You

1958 *KING CREOLE:*
SIDE 1: King Creole; As Long As I Have You; Hard Headed Woman; Trouble; Dixieland Rock
SIDE 2: Don't Ask Me Why; Lover Doll; Crawfish; Young Dreams; Steadfast, Loyal And True; New Orleans

1958 *ELVIS CHRISTMAS ALBUM:*
compiled from the EPs: *Peace In The Valley, Elvis Sings Christmas Songs* and *Christmas With Elvis*

1959 *FOR LP FANS ONLY:*
SIDE 1: That's All Right (Mama); Lawdy, Miss Clawdy; Mystery Train; Playing For Keeps; Poor Boy
SIDE 2: My Baby Left Me; I Was The One; Shake, Rattle And Roll; I'm Left, You're Right, She's Gone; You're A Heartbreaker

1959   *ELVIS SAILS:*
       SIDE 1: Press interview with Elvis Presley
       SIDE 2: Elvis Presley's Newsreel interview; Pat Hernon
       interviews Elvis

1959   *A DATE WITH ELVIS:*
       SIDE 1: Blue Moon Of Kentucky; Young And Beautiful;
       Baby, I Don't Care; Milkcow Blues Boogie; Baby, Let's
       Play House
       SIDE 2: Good Rocking Tonight; Is It So Strange; We're
       Gonna Move; I Want To Be Free; I Forgot To
       Remember To Forget

1959   *50,000,000 ELVIS FANS CAN'T BE WRONG (GOLDEN
       RECORDS VOL.2):*
       SIDE 1: I Need Your Love Tonight; Don't; Wear My Ring
       Around Your Neck; My Wish Came True; I Got Stung
       SIDE 2: One Night; A Big Hunk O' Love; I Beg Of You; A
       Fool Such As I; Don'cha Think It's Time?

1960   *ELVIS IS BACK:*
       SIDE 1: Make Me Know It; Fever; The Girl Of My Best
       Friend; I Will Be Home Again; Dirty, Dirty Feeling; The
       Thrill Of Your Love
       SIDE 2: Soldier Boy; Such A Night; It Feels So Right;
       The Girl Next Door Went A' Walking; Like A Baby;
       Reconsider Baby

1960 *G.I. BLUES:*
SIDE 1: Tonight Is So Right For Love; What's She Really Like?; Frankfurt Special; Wooden Heart; G.I. Blues
SIDE 2: Pocketful Of Rainbows; Shoppin' Around; Big Boots; Didja' Ever; Blue Suede Shoes; Doin' The Best I Can

1960 *FLAMING STAR:*
SIDE 1: Flaming Star; Wonderful World; Night Life; All I Need Was The Rain; Too Much Monkey Business
SIDE 2: Yellow Rose Of Texas / The Eyes Of Texas; She's A Machine; Do The Vega; Tiger Man

1960 *HIS HAND IN MINE:*
SIDE 1: His Hand In Mine; I'm Gonna Walk Dem Golden Stairs; In My Father's House; Milky White Way; Know Only Him; I Believe In The Man In The Sky
SIDE 2: Joshua Fit The Battle; Jesus Knows What I Need; Swing Down Sweet Chariot; Mansion Over The Hilltop; If We Never Meet Again; Working On The Building

1961 *SOMETHING FOR EVERYBODY:*
SIDE 1: There's Always Me; Give Me The Right; It's A Sin; Sentimental Me; Starting Today; Gently
SIDE 2: I'm Comin' Home; In Your Arms; Put The Blame On Me; Judy; I Want You With Me; I Slipped, I Stumbled, I Fell

1961 *BLUE HAWAII:*
SIDE 1: Blue Hawaii; Almost Always True; Aloha-Oe;
No More; Can't Help Falling In Love; Rock-A-Hula
Baby; Moonlight Swim
SIDE 2: Ku-U-I-Po (Hawaiian Sweetheart); Ito Eats;
Slicin' Sand; Hawaiian Sunset; Beach Boy Blues;
Island Of Love; Hawaiian Wedding Song

1962 *POT LUCK:*
SIDE 1: Kiss Me Quick; Just For Old Times' Sake;
Gonna Get Back Home Somehow; (Such An) Easy
Question; Steppin' Out Of Line; I'm Yours
SIDE 2: Something Blue; Suspicion; I Feel That I've
Known You Forever; Night Rider; Fountain Of Love;
That's Someone You Never Forget

1962 *GIRLS! GIRLS! GIRLS!:*
SIDE 1: Girls! Girls! Girls!; I Don't Wanna Be Tied;
Where Do You Come From; I Don't Want To; We'll Be
Together; A Boy Like Me, A Girl Like You; Earth Boy
SIDE 2: Return To Sender; Because Of Love; Thanks To
The Rolling Sea; Song Of The Shrimps; The Walls
Have Ears; We're Comin' In Loaded

1963 *IT HAPPENED AT THE WORLD'S FAIR:*
SIDE 1: Beyond The Bend; Relax; Take Me To The Fair;
They Remind Me Too Much Of You; One Broken
Heart For Sale
SIDE 2: I'm Falling In Love Tonight; Cotton Candy
Land; A World Of Our Own; How Would You Like To
Be?; Happy Ending

1963   *ELVIS GOLDEN RECORDS VOL. 3:*
SIDE 1: It's Now Or Never; Stuck On You; Fame And
Fortune; I Gotta Know; Surrender; I Feel So Bad
SIDE 2: Are You Lonesome Tonight?; (Marie's The
Name) His Latest Flame; Little Sister; Good Luck
Charm; Anything That's Part Of You; She's Not You

1963   *FUN IN ACAPULCO:*
SIDE 1: Fun In Acapulco; Vino, Dinero Y Amor;
Mexico; El Toro; Marguerita; The Bullfighter Was A
Lady; (There's) No Room To Rhumba In A Sports Car
SIDE 2: I Think I'm Gonna Like It Here; Bossa Nova
Baby; You Can Say No In Acapulco; Guadalajara;
Love Me Tonight; Slowly, But Surely

1964   *KISSIN' COUSINS:*
SIDE 1: Kissin' Cousins (No.2); Smokey Mountain Boy;
There's Gold In The Mountains; One Boy, Two Little
Girls; Catchin' On Fast; Tender Feeling
SIDE 2: Anyone (Could Fall In Love With You);
Barefoot Ballad; Once Is Enough; Kissin' Cousins;
Echoes Of Love; (It's A) Long Lonely Highway

1964   *ROUSTABOUT:*
SIDE 1: Roustabout; Little Egypt; Poison Ivy League;
Hard Knocks; It's A Wonderful World; Big Love
SIDE 2: One Track Heart; It's Carnival Time; Carny
Town; There's A Brand New Day On The Horizon;
Wheels On My Heels

1965   *GIRL HAPPY:*
SIDE 1: Girl Happy; Spring Fever; Fort Lauderdale
Chamber Of Commerce; Startin' Tonight; Wolf Call;
Do Not Disturb
SIDE 2: Cross My Heart And Hope To Die; The
Meanest Girl In Town; Do The Clam; Puppet On A
String; I've Got To Find My Baby; You'll Be Gone

1965   *ELVIS FOR EVERYONE:*
SIDE 1: Your Cheatin' Heart; Summer Kisses, Winter
Tears; Finders Keepers, Losers Weepers; In My Way;
Tomorrow Night; Memphis, Tennessee
SIDE 2: For The Millionth And The Last Time; Forget
Me Never; Sound Advice; Santa Lucia; I Met Her
Today; When It Rains, It Really Pours

1965   *HAREM HEAVEN / HARUM SCARUM (IN USA):*
SIDE 1: Harum Scarum; My Desert Serenade; Go East
Young Man; Mirage; Kismet; Shake That Tambourine
SIDE 2: Hey, Little Girl; Golden Coins; So Close, Yet So
Far; Animal Instinct; Wisdom Of The Ages

1966   *FRANKIE AND JOHNNY:*
SIDE 1: Frankie And Johnny; Come Along; Petunia,
The Gardener's Daughter; Chesay; What Every
Woman Lives For; Look Out Broadway
SIDE 2: Beginner's Luck; Down By The Riverside /
When The Saints Go Marching In; Shout It Out;
Hard Luck; Please Don't Stop Loving Me; Everybody
Come Aboard

1966   *PARADISE, HAWAIIAN STYLE:*
SIDE 1: Paradise, Hawaiian Style; Queenie Wahine's
Papaya; Scratch My Back; Drums Of The Islands;
Datin'
SIDE 2: A Dog's Life; Stop Where You Are; This Is My
Heaven; Sand Castle

1966   *CALIFORNIA HOLIDAY / SPINOUT (IN USA):*
SIDE 1: Stop, Look And Listen; Adam And Eve; All That
I Am; Never Say Yes; Am I Ready; Beach Shark
SIDE 2: Spinout; Smorgasbord; I'll Be Back;
Tomorrow Is A Long Time; Down In The Alley; I'll
Remember You

1967   *HOW GREAT THOU ART:*
SIDE 1: How Great Thou Art; In The Garden;
Something Bigger; Father Along; Stand By Me;
Without Him
SIDE 2: So High; Where Could I Go But To The Lord;
By And By; If The Lord Wasn't Walking By My Side;
Run On; Where No One Stands Alone; Crying In The
Chapel

1967   *DOUBLE TROUBLE:*
SIDE 1: Double Trouble; Baby, If You'll Give Me All Of
Your Love; Could I Fall In Love; Long-Legged Girl; City
By Night; Old MacDonald
SIDE 2: I Love Only One Girl; There Is So Much World
To See; It Won't be Long; Never Ending; Blue River;
What Now, What Next, Where To?

1967   *CLAMBAKE:*
        SIDE 1: Guitar Man; Clambake; Who Needs Money?;
        A House That Has Everything; Confidence; Hey,
        Hey, Hey
        SIDE 2: You Don't Know Me; The Girl I Never Loved;
        How Can You Lose What You Never Had?; Big Boss
        Man; Singing Tree; Just Call Me Lonesome

1968   *ELVIS GOLDEN RECORDS VOL. 4:*
        SIDE 1: Love Letters; Witchcraft; It Hurts Me; What'd
        I Say?; Please Don't Drag That String Around;
        Indescribably Blue
        SIDE 2: (You're The) Devil In Disguise; Lonely Man; A
        Mess Of Blues; Ask Me; Ain't That Loving You,
        Baby?; Just Tell Her Jim Said Hello

1968   *SPEEDWAY:*
        SIDE 1: Speedway; There Ain't Nothing Like A Song;
        Your Time Hasn't Come Yet, Baby; Who Are You?;
        He's Your Uncle, Not Your Dad; Let Yourself Go
        SIDE 2: Your Groovy Self; Five Sleepy Heads;
        Western Union; Mine; Goin' Home; Suppose

1968   *'68 COMEBACK SPECIAL:*
        SIDE 1: Trouble; Guitar Man; Lawdy, Miss Clawdy;
        Baby, What You Want Me To Do?; Dialogue;
        Heartbreak Hotel; Hound Dog; All Shook Up; Can't
        Help Falling In Love; Jailhouse Rock; Love Me
        Tender

SIDE 2: Where Could I Go But To The Lord?; Up Above My Head; Saved; Dialogue; Blue Christmas; One Night; Memories; Nothingville; Dialogue???; Big Boss Man; Guitar Man; Little Egypt; Trouble; Guitar Man; If I Can Dream

1969 *FROM ELVIS IN MEMPHIS:*
SIDE 1: Wearin' That Loved On Look; Only The Strong Survive; I'll Hold You In My Arms; Long Black Limousine; It Keeps Right On A'Hurtin'; I'm Movin' On
SIDE 2: Power Of My Love; Gentle On My Mind; After Loving You; True Love Travels On A Gravel Road; Any Day Now; In The Ghetto

1969 *ELVIS - FROM MEMPHIS TO VEGAS:*
SIDE 1: Blue Suede Shoes; Johnny B. Goode; All Shook Up; Are You Lonesome Tonight?; Hound Dog; I Can't Stop Loving You; My Babe
SIDE 2: Mystery Train; Tiger Man; Words; In The Ghetto; Suspicious Minds; Can't Help Falling In Love; From Vegas To Memphis
SIDE 3: Inherit The Wind; This Is The Story; Stranger In My Own Home Town; A Little Bit Of Green; And The Grass Won't Pay No Mind
SIDE 4: Do You Know Who I Am; From A Jack To A King; The Fair's Moving On; You'll Think Of Me; Without Love (There Is Nothing)

1970   *LET'S BE FRIENDS:*
       SIDE 1: Stay Away Joe; I'm A Fool; Let's Be Friends;
       Let's Forget About The Stars; Mama
       SIDE 2: I'll Be There; Almost; Change Of Habit;
       Have A Happy

1970   *ON STAGE – FEBRUARY 1970:*
       SIDE 1: See See Rider; Release Me; Sweet Caroline;
       Runaway; The Wonder Of You
       SIDE 2: Polk Salad Annie; Yesterday; Proud Mary; Walk A
       Mile In My Shoes; Let It Be Me

1970   *WORLDWIDE 50 GOLD AWARD HITS, VOL. 1:*
       SIDE 1: Heartbreak Hotel; I Was The One; I Want You, I
       Need You, I Love You; Don't Be Cruel; Hound Dog; Love
       Me Tender
       SIDE 2: Anyway You Want Me; Too Much; Playing For
       Keeps; All Shook Up; That's When Your Heartaches
       Begin; Loving You
       SIDE 3: (Let Me Be Your) Teddy Bear; Jailhouse Rock; Treat
       Me Nice; I Beg Of You; Don't; Wear My Ring Around
       Your Neck; Hard-Headed Woman
       SIDE 4: I Got Stung; (Now And There's) A Fool Such As I;
       A Big Hunk O' Love; Stuck On You; A Mess Of Blues; It's
       Now Or Never
       SIDE 5: I Gotta Know; Are You Lonesome Tonight?;
       Surrender; I Feel So Bad; Little Sister; Can't Help Falling
       In Love

SIDE 6: Rock-A-Hula Baby; Anything That's Part Of You; Good Luck Charm; She's Not You; Return To Sender; Where Do You Come From?; One Broken Heart For Sale
SIDE 7: (You're The) Devil In Disguise; Bossa Nova Baby; Kissin' Cousins; Viva Las Vegas; Ain't That Loving You Baby; Wooden Heart
SIDE 8: Crying In The Chapel; If I Can Dream; In The Ghetto; Suspicious Minds; Don't Cry Daddy; Kentucky Rain; Excerpts From *Elvis Sails* Interview

1970   *ALMOST IN LOVE:*
SIDE 1: Almost In Love; Long-Legged Girl; Edge Of Reality; My Little Girl; A Little Less Conversation
SIDE 2: Rubberneckin'; Clean Up Your Own Back Yard; U.S. Male; Charro; Stay Away Joe

1970   *ELVIS CHRISTMAS ALBUM:*
SIDE 1: Blue Christmas; Silent Night; White Christmas; Santa Claus Is Back In Town; I'll Be Home For Christmas
SIDE 2: If Every Day Was Like Christmas; Here Comes Santa Claus; O Little Town Of Bethlehem; Santa, Bring My Baby Back; Mama Liked The Roses

1970   *ELVIS IN PERSON AT THE INTERNATIONAL HOTEL, LAS VEGAS, NEVADA* – RECORDED IN JULY AND AUGUST 1969:
SIDE 1: Blue Suede Shoes; Johnny B. Goode; All Shook Up; Are You Lonesome Tonight?; Hound Dog; I Can't Stop Loving You; My Babe

SIDE 2: Mystery Train; Tiger Man; Words; In The
Ghetto; Suspicious Minds; Can't Help Falling In
Love

1970   *BACK IN MEMPHIS:*
SIDE 1: Inherit The Wind; This is The Story; Stranger
In My Own Home Town; A Little Bit Of Green; And
The Grass Won't Pay No Mind
SIDE 2: Do You Know Who I Am?; From A Jack To a
King; The Fair's Moving On; You'll Think Of Me;
Without Love (There Is Nothing)

1970   *ELVIS – THAT'S THE WAY IT IS:*
SIDE 1: I Just Can't Help Believin'; Twenty Days And
Twenty Nights; How The Web Was Woven; Patch It
Up; Mary In The Morning; You Don't Have To Say
You Love Me
SIDE 2: You've Lost That Lovin' Feeling; I've Lost You;
Just Pretend; Stranger In The Crowd; The Next Step
Is Love; Bridge Over Troubled Water

1971   *I'M 10,000 YEARS OLD, ELVIS COUNTRY:*
SIDE 1: Snowbird; Tomorrow Never Comes; Little
Cabin On The Hill; Whole Lotta Shakin' Goin' On;
Funny How Time Slips Away; I Really Don't Want To
Know
SIDE 2: There Goes My Everything; It's Your Baby,
You Rock It; The Fool; Faded Love; I Washed My
Hands In Muddy Water; Make The World Go Away

1971   *YOU'LL NEVER WALK ALONE:*
        SIDE 1: You'll Never Walk Alone; Who Am I?; Let Us
        Pray; (There'll Be) Peace In The Valley; We Call On
        Him
        SIDE 2: I Believe; It Is No Secret (What God Can Do);
        Sing You Children; Take My Hand, Precious Lord

1971   *LOVE LETTERS FROM ELVIS:*
        SIDE 1: Love Letters; When I'm Over You; If I Were
        You; Got My Mojo Working; Heart Of Rome
        SIDE 2: Only Believe; This Is Our Dance; Cindy, Cindy;
        I'll Never Know; It Ain't No Big Thing (But It's
        Growing); Life

1971   *C'MON EVERYBODY:*
        SIDE 1: C'mon Everybody; Angel; Easy Come, Easy Go;
        A Whistling Tune; Follow That Dream
        SIDE 2: King Of The Whole Wide World; I'll Take Love;
        Today, Tomorrow And Forever; I'm Not The Marrying
        Kind; This Is Living

1971   *ELVIS: THE OTHER SIDES – WORLDWIDE GOLD AWARDS
        HITS, VOL. 2:*
        SIDE 1: Puppet On A String; Witchcraft; Trouble; Poor
        Boy; I Want To Be Free; Doncha' Think It's Time?;
        Young Dreams
        SIDE 2: The Next Step Is Love; You Don't Have To Say
        You Love Me; Paralyzed; My Wish Came True; When
        My Blue Moon Turns To Gold Again; Lonesome
        Cowboy

SIDE 3: My Baby Left Me; It Hurts Me; I Need Your Love Tonight; Tell Me Why; Please Don't Drag That String Around; Young And Beautiful
SIDE 4: Hot Dog; New Orleans; We're Gonna Move; Crawfish; King Creole; I Believe In The Man In The Sky; Dixieland Rock
SIDE 5: The Wonder Of You; They Remind Me Too Much Of You; Mean Woman Blues; Lonely Man; Any Day Now; Don't Ask Me Why
SIDE 6: (Marie's The Name) His Latest Flame; I Really Don't Want To Know; (You're So Square) Baby I Don't Care; I've Lost You; Let Me; Love Me;
SIDE 7: Got A Lot O' Livin' To Do; Fame And Fortune; Rip It Up; There Goes My Everything; Lover Doll; One Night
SIDE 8: Just Tell Her Jim Said Hello; Ask Me; Patch It Up; As Long As I Have You; You'll Think Of Me; Wild In The Country

1971 *I GOT LUCKY:*
SIDE 1: I Got Lucky; What A Wonderful World; I Need Somebody To Lean On; Yoga Is As Yoga Does; Riding The Rainbow
SIDE 2: Fools Fall In Love; The Love Machine; Home Is Where The Heart Is; You Gotta Stop; If You Think I Don't Need You

1971   *ELVIS SINGS THE WONDERFUL WORLD OF CHRISTMAS:*
        SIDE 1: O Come All Ye Faithful; The First Noël; On A
        Snowy Christmas Night; Winter Wonderland; The
        Wonderful World Of Christmas; It Won't Seem Like
        Christmas (Without You)
        SIDE 2: I'll Be Home For Christmas Day; I'll Get Home
        On Christmas Day; Holly Leaves And Christmas
        Trees; Merry Christmas, Baby; Silver Bells

1972   *ELVIS NOW:*
        SIDE 1: Help Me Make It Through The Night; Miracle
        Of The Rosary; Hey Jude; Put Your Hand In The
        Hand; Until It's Time For You To Go
        SIDE 2: We Can Make The Morning; Early Mornin'
        Rain; Sylvia; Fools Rush In; I Was Born About Ten
        Thousand Years Ago

1972   *HE TOUCHED ME:*
        SIDE 1: He Touched Me; I've Got Confidence;
        Amazing Grace; Seeing Is Believing; He Is My
        Everything; Bosom Of Abraham
        SIDE 2: An Evening Prayer; Lead Me, Guide Me; There
        Is No God But God; A Thing Called Love; I, John;
        Reach Out To Jesus

1972   *ELVIS AS RECORDED AT MADISON SQUARE GARDEN:*
        SIDE 1: Introduction: Also Sprach Zarathustra; That's
        All Right (Mama); Proud Mary; Never Been To Spain;
        You Don't Have To Say You Love Me; You Lost That

Lovin' Feelin'; Polk Salad Annie; Love Me; All Shook
Up; Heartbreak Hotel; Medley: (Let Me Be Your)
Teddy Bear, Don't Be Cruel; Love Me Tender
SIDE 2: Impossible Dream; Introduction by Elvis;
Hound Dog; Suspicious Minds; For The Good
Times; American Trilogy; Funny How Time Slips
Away; I Can't Stop Loving You; Can't Help Falling In
Love; End Theme

1972   *ELVIS SINGS HITS FROM HIS MOVIES, VOL. 1:*
SIDE 1: Down By the Riverside / When The Saints
Go Marching In; They Remind Me Too Much Of
You; Confidence; Frankie And Johnny; Guitar Man
SIDE 2: Long-Legged Girl (With The Short Dress On);
You Don't Know Me; How Would You Like To Be?;
Big Boss Man; Old MacDonald

1972   *BURNING LOVE AND HITS FROM HIS MOVIES, VOL.·2:*
SIDE 1: Burning Love; Tender Feeling; Am I Ready?;
Tonight Is So Right For Love; Guadalajara
SIDE 2: It's A Matter Of Time; No More; Santa Lucia;
We'll Be Together; I Love Only One Girl

1973   *SEPARATE WAYS:*
SIDE 1: Separate Ways; Sentimental Me; In My Way;
I Met Her Today; What Now, What Next, Where To?
SIDE 2: Always On My Mind; I Slipped, I Stumbled, I
Fell; Is It So Strange?; Forget Me Never; Old Shep

1973   ALOHA FROM HAWAII VIA SATELLITE:
        SIDE 1: Introduction/Also Sprach Zarathustra; See
        See Rider; Burning Love; Something; You Gave Me A
        Mountain; Steamroller Blues
        SIDE 2: My Way; Love Me; Johnny B. Goode; It's Over;
        Blue Suede Shoes; I'm So Lonesome I Could Cry
        SIDE 3: What Now My Love?; Fever; Welcome To My
        World; Suspicious Minds; Introduction By Elvis
        SIDE 4: I'll Remember You; Medley: Long Tall Sally,
        Whole Lotta Shakin' Goin' On; American Trilogy; A
        Big Hunk O' Love; Can't Help Falling In Love; Closing
        Vamp

1973   *ALMOST IN LOVE:*
        SIDE 1: Almost In Love; Long-Legged Girl; Edge Of
        Reality; My Little Friend; A Little Less Conversation
        SIDE 2: Rubberneckin'; Clean Up Your Own Backyard;
        U.S. Male; Charro; Stay Away

1973   *ELVIS:*
        SIDE 1: Fool; Where Do I Go From Here?; Love Me,
        Love The Life I Lead; It's Still Here; It's Impossible
        SIDE 2: For Lovin' Me; Padre; I'll Take You Home
        Again, Kathleen; I Will Be True; Don't Think Twice,
        It's All Right

1973   *RAISED ON ROCK:*
        SIDE 1: Raised On Rock; Are You Sincere?; Find Out
        What's Happening; I Miss You; Girl Of Mine

SIDE 2: For Ol' Times' Sake; If You Don't Come Back; Just A Little Bit; Sweet Angeline; Three Corn Patches

1974 *ELVIS – A LEGENDARY PERFORMER, VOL. 1:*
SIDE 1: That's All Right (Mama); I Love You Because; Heartbreak Hotel; Excerpt From 'Elvis Sails' Interview; Don't Be Cruel; Love Me; Trying To Get To You
SIDE 2: Love Me Tender; (There'll Be) Peace In The Valley (For Me); Excerpts From 'Elvis Sails' Interview; (Now And Then There's) A Fool Such As I; Tonight's All Right For Love; Are You Lonesome Tonight?; Can't Help Falling In Love

1974 *GOOD TIMES:*
SIDE 1: Take Good Care Of Her; Loving Arms; I Got A Feelin' In My Body; If That Isn't Love; She Wears My Ring
SIDE 2: I've Got A Thing About You, Baby; My Boy; Spanish Eyes; Talk About The Good Times; Good Times Charlie's Got The Blues

1974 *RECORDED LIVE ON STAGE IN MEMPHIS:*
SIDE 1: See See Rider; I Got A Woman; Love Me; Trying To Get To You; Medley: Long Tall Sally; Whole Lotta Shakin' Goin' On; Your Mama Don't Dance; Flip, Flop And Fly; Jailhouse Rock; Hound Dog; Why Me Lord?; How Great Thou Art

SIDE 2: Blueberry Hill; I Can't Stop Loving You; Help Me; An American Trilogy; Let Me Be There; My Baby Left Me; Lawdy, Miss Clawdy; Can't Help Falling In Love; Closing Vamp

1974   *HAVING FUN WITH ELVIS ON STAGE* (interviews only)

1975   *PROMISED LAND:*
SIDE 1: Promised Land; There's A Honky Tonk Angel (Who'll Take Me Back In); Help Me; Mr. Songman; Love Song Of The Year
SIDE 2: It's Midnight; Your Love's Been A Long Time Coming; If You Talk In Your Sleep; Thinking About You; You Ask Me To

1975   *PURE GOLD:*
SIDE 1: Kentucky Rain; Fever; It's Impossible; Jailhouse Rock; Don't Be Cruel
SIDE 2: I Got A Woman; All Shook Up; Loving You; In The Ghetto; Love Me Tender

1975   *ELVIS TODAY:*
SIDE 1: T-R-O-U-B-L-E; And I Love You So; Susan When She Tried; Woman Without Love; Shake A Hand
SIDE 2: Pieces Of My Life; Fairytale; I Can Help; Bringing It Back; Green Green Grass Of Home

1975   *THE SUN SESSIONS:*
SIDE 1: That's All Right; Blue Moon Of Kentucky; I
Don't Care If The Sun Don't Shine; Good Rockin'
Tonight; Milkcow Blues Boogie; You're A
Heartbreaker; I'm Left, You're Right, She's Gone;
Baby, Let's Play House
SIDE 2: Mystery Train; I Forgot To Remember To
Forget; I'll Never Let You Go (Little Darlin'); I Love
You Because; Trying To Get To You; Blue Moon; Just
Because; I Love You Because (2nd version)

1976   *ELVIS – A LEGENDARY PERFORMER, VOL. 2:*
SIDE 1: Harbor Lights; Interview With Elvis – Jay
Thompson, Wichita Falls, Texas, April 10, 1956;
I Want You, I Need You, I Love You; Blue Christmas;
Jailhouse Rock; It's Now Or Never
SIDE 2: A Cane And A High Starched Collar;
Presentation Of Awards To Elvis (Pearl Harbor,
Hawaii, 25 March 1961); Blue Hawaii; Such A Night;
Baby, What You Want Me To Do; How Great Thou
Art

1976   *FROM ELVIS PRESLEY BOULEVARD, MEMPHIS, TENNESSEE:*
SIDE 1: Hurt; Never Again; Blue Eyes Crying In The
Rain; Danny Boy; The Last Farewell
SIDE 2: For The Heart; Bitter They Are, Harder They
Fall; Solitaire; Love Coming Down; I'll Never Fall In
Love Again

1976   *FRANKIE AND JOHNNY:*
        SIDE 1: Frankie And Johnny; Come Along; What Every
        Woman Lives For; Hard Luck; Please Don't Stop
        Loving Me
        SIDE 2: Down By The Riverside; When The Saints Go
        Marching In; Petunia, The Gardener's Daughter;
        Beginner's Luck; Shout It Out

1977   *WELCOME TO MY WORLD:*
        SIDE 1: Welcome To My World; Help Me Make It
        Through The Night; Release Me; I Really Don't Want
        To Know; For The Good Times
        SIDE 2: Make The World Go Away; Gentle On My
        Mind; I'm So Lonesome I Could Cry; Your Cheatin'
        Heart; I Can't Stop Loving You

1977   *MOODY BLUE:*
        SIDE 1: Unchained Melody; If You Love Me; Little
        Darlin'; He'll Have To Go; Let Me Be There
        SIDE 2: Way Down; Pledging My Love; Moody Blue;
        She Thinks I Still Care; It's Easy For You

1977   *ELVIS IN CONCERT:*
        Elvis Fans' Comments/Opening Riff; Also Sprach
        Zarathustra; See See Rider; That's All Right; Are You
        Lonesome Tonight?; (Let Me Be Your) Teddy
        Bear/Don't Be Cruel; Elvis Fans' Comments II; You
        Gave Me A Mountain; Jailhouse Rock; Elvis Fans'
        Comments III; How Great Thou Art; Elvis Fans'
        Comments IV; I Really Don't Want To Know; Elvis

Introduces His Father; Hurt; Hound Dog; My Way; Can't Help Falling In Love; Closing Riff / Special Message From Elvis's Father; I Got A Woman / Amen; Elvis Talks; Love Me; If You Love Me (Let Me Know); O Sole Mio / It's Now Or Never; Trying To Get To You; Hawaiian Wedding Song; Fairytale; Little Sister; Early Morning Rain; What'd I Say; Johnny B. Goode; And I Love You So

RECORDED AT TWO SHOWS ON 19 AND 21 JUNE 1977, RELEASED IN OCTOBER AFTER HIS DEATH.

ELVIS MOVIES/VIDEOS/DVDs

1956   *LOVE ME TENDER*

1957   *LOVING YOU*

1957   *JAILHOUSE ROCK*

1958   *KING CREOLE*

1960   *G.I. BLUES*

1960   *FLAMING STAR*

1961   *WILD IN THE COUNTRY*

1961   *BLUE HAWAII*

1962   *FOLLOW THAT DREAM*

1962   *KID GALAHAD*

1962   *GIRLS! GIRLS! GIRLS!*

1963   *IT HAPPENED AT THE WORLD'S FAIR*

1963   *FUN IN ACAPULCO*

1964   *KISSIN' COUSINS*

1964   *VIVA LAS VEGAS*

1964   *ROUSTABOUT*

1965   *GIRL HAPPY*

1965   *TICKLE ME*

1965   *HAREM HOLIDAY* (*HARUM SCARUM* in USA)

1966   *FRANKIE AND JOHNNY*

1966   *PARADISE, HAWAIIAN STYLE*

1966   *CALIFORNIA HOLIDAY* (*SPINOUT* in USA)

1967   *EASY COME, EASY GO*

1967   *DOUBLE TROUBLE*

1967   *CLAMBAKE*

1967   *STAY AWAY, JOE*

1968   *SPEEDWAY*

1968   *LIVE A LITTLE, LOVE A LITTLE*

1968   '*68 COMEBACK SPECIAL* or *ELVIS PRESLEY SHOW '68*:
       Video cassette and DVD Tracks as on LP;
       recorded live 3 December 1968

1969   *CHARRO!* (first non-musical role)

1969 *THE TROUBLE WITH GIRLS*

1969 *CHANGE OF HABIT*

1970 *ELVIS: THAT'S THE WAY IT IS*
Video cassette and DVD; tracks as for LP

1972 *ELVIS ON TOUR*:
Johnny B Goode; See See Rider; Polk Salad Annie.;
Separate Ways; Proud Mary; Burning Love; Don't Be
Cruel; Ready Teddy; That's All Right; Lead Me, Guide
Me; Bosom Of Abraham; Love Me Tender; Until It's
Time For You To Go; Suspicious Minds; I, John;
Bridge Over Troubled Water; Funny How Time Slips
Away; An American Trilogy (Dixie, All My Trials,
Battle Hymn Of The Republic); Mystery Train; I Got
A Woman; Amen; A Big Hunk O' Love; You Gave Me
A Mountain; Lawdy, Miss Clawdy; Can't Help
Falling In Love; Memories

1973 *ALOHA FROM HAWAII*:
Video cassette and DVD; tracks as for LP

1977 *ELVIS IN CONCERT*:
Video cassette and DVD; tracks as for LP

1981 *THIS IS ELVIS PART 1:* Video cassette and DVD
(Marie's The Name) His Latest Flame; Moody Blue;
That's All Right; Shake, Rattle And Roll; Flip Flop
And Fly; Heartbreak Hotel; Hound Dog; Excerpt
from Hy Gardner Interview; My Baby Left Me;

Merry Christmas Baby; Mean Woman Blues; Don't Be Cruel; (Let Me Be Your) Teddy Bear; Jailhouse Rock; Army Swearing In; G.I. Blues; Excerpt from 'Departure For Germany' press conference; Excerpt from 'Home From Germany' press conference

1981 *THIS IS ELVIS PART 2:*
Video cassette and DVD
Too Much Monkey Business; Love Me Tender; I've Got A Thing About You Baby; I Need Your Love Tonight; Blue Suede Shoes; Viva Las Vegas; Excerpt from the 'Madison Square Garden' press conference; Excerpt from the;Madison Square Garden' press conference; Are You Lonesome Tonight?; My Way; An American Trilogy; Memories; Suspicious Minds; Excerpt from JC's Award to Elvis; Promised Land

1987 *ELVIS 56 IN THE BEGINNING:*
Video cassette and DVD
My Way; Baby What You Want Me To Do; Blue Suede Shoes; Good Rockin' Tonight; Heartbreak Hotel; Shake Rattle and Roll; Baby, Let's Play House; Tutti Frutti; My Baby Left Me; Blue Moon; Hound Dog; He's Only a Prayer Away; Lawdy, Miss Clawdy; Don't Be Cruel; Trying To Get To You; Anyway You Want Me; Ready Teddy; Love Me Tender; Peace in the Valley; Love Me

Biographical film narrated by Levon Helm

1988   *ONE NIGHT WITH YOU*:
        Video cassette and DVD
        That's All Right; Heartbreak Hotel; Love Me; Baby,
        What You Want Me to Do; Blue Suede Shoes;
        Lawdy, Miss Clawdy; When My Blue Moon Turns to
        Gold Again; Blue Christmas; Trying To Get To You;
        One Night; Memories

1992   *THE LOST PERFORMANCES*:
        Video cassette and DVD
        The Wonder Of You, Heartbreak Hotel, Hound Dog,
        Don't Be Cruel and Don't Cry Daddy. Elvis sings a
        powerful In The Ghetto and an emotional Make
        The World Go Away. I Was The One; Baby Let's Play
        House; Don't; Money Honey; All Shook Up; Medley:
        Teddy Bear / Don't Be Cruel; Are You Lonesome
        Tonight?; I Can't Stop Loving You; How Great Thou
        Art; Release Me; I Can't Stop Loving You (over
        credits)

        OUTTAKES FROM LIVE CONCERT PERFORMANCES
        FILMED IN 1970 AND 1972 FOR THE FILMS *THAT'S
        THE WAY IT IS* AND *ELVIS ON TOUR*

❝Till we meet you again, may God bless you. Adios.❞
1977, AT THE END OF A CONCERT DURING HIS LAST TOUR